Responses to 101 Questions on the Psalms and Other Writings

Roland E. Murphy, O. Carm.

PAULIST PRESS
New York / Mahwah, N.J.

Cover designs for this series are by James Brisson Design & Production, Williamsville, Vermont

The transliteration of Hebrew words is made in a simplified form for the sake of readers' pronunciation.

Library of Congress Cataloging-in-Publication Data

Murphy, Roland Edmund, 1917-
     Responses to 101 questions on the Psalms and other writings / by Roland E. Murphy.
          p.   cm.
     ISBN 0-8091-3526-4 (paper)
     1. Bible.   O.T. Hagiographa—Criticism, interpretation, etc.—Miscellanea.
     I. Title.
BS1308.M87   1994   94-3739
221'.042—dc20   CIP
                                                                     AC

Published by Paulist Press
997 Macarthur Boulevard
Mahwah, NJ 07430

Printed and bound in the
United States of America

CONTENTS

PROVERBS

JOB

SONG OF SONGS

DANIEL AND APOCALYPTIC

CONCLUSION

ABBREVIATIONS

ANET J.B. Pritchard (ed.) *Ancient Near Eastern Texts* (Princeton University Press, 1950; 3d ed. with supplement, 1978)

MT Masoretic text

NAB *New American Bible*

NEB *New English Bible*

NJV *New Jewish Version*

NRSV *New Revised Standard Version*

RSV *Revised Standard Version*

WBC Word Biblical Commentary

FOREWORD

At an annual meeting of the Society of Biblical Literature, I walked past the Paulist Press exhibit booth and the indefatigable editor, Fr. Lawrence Boadt, C.S.P., pointed to a series of *101 Responses*, and asked, "Why don't you do a volume on the Writings?" It did not take me long to get caught up with this final section of the Hebrew Bible, that runs the gamut from the very familiar (Psalms) to the exotic (Esther). Although it was the last part of the Hebrew Bible to take shape, it included masterpieces (Job) and more humble works (Chronicles).

Some of these "responses" are things I forgot to say, while others are expressed in better, "cleaner" language. Every lecturer remembers missed opportunities: "If only I had thought of that response at the time!" The questions are a distillation of some forty years in lecture halls, weekend workshops and week-long institutes. These may not be the cream of the crop; they have been filtered through experience and judgment as to what is more important. The value of this little book is that it enables the author to be more exact, less rambling, in reply to questions.

Perhaps the most profitable way of utilizing this text is to read the biblical work in question, and then go to the series of responses. There are references to the biblical text along the way, so that it aims to be Bible-centered. There was no sense in adding a bibliography at the end, since this would be easily available in the *New Jerome Biblical Commentary* or other sources. The questions that readers do or do not ask are often an indication of the manner in which they have read the biblical work, actively or passively. These responses presuppose that the pertinent book has been read—aggressively.

DEDICATED TO ALL WHO LISTENED AND QUESTIONED

THE 101 QUESTIONS AND RESPONSES

Q. 1. What do you mean by the "Writings"?

The term "Writings" (in Hebrew *kethuvim*) refers to the third and last part of the Hebrew Bible according to Jewish tradition. The first two parts are the "law" (*Torâ*) and the "prophets" (*Nevi'im*), and they are mentioned in the New Testament (Matt 7:12; Luke 16:16; Acts 13:15). The tripartite division of the Jewish Bible was already indicated in the Greek prologue to Ecclesiasticus (or Sirach). Sirach's grandson translated the work of his grandfather, Ben Sira, into Greek sometime after 132 B.C. In his prologue he speaks of "the law, the prophets, and the later authors"—an indication that the Hebrew Bible was already assuming this form before the time of Christ. An acronym has been formed from the first letters of the three Hebrew words: Tanak, standing for Torah, Nevi'im and Kethuvim. In 1988 the Jewish Publication Society published a new translation of the Hebrew Bible entitled *Tanakh: The Holy Scriptures*.

The Writings are found also in the Christian Bible, but not under that name. The division of the Christian Bible is fourfold: laws (Pentateuch), histories, poetical books and prophets. This division ultimately goes back to the Greek translation of the Hebrew Bible, the so-called Septuagint, that was made in the third and second centuries immediately preceding the Christian era. Neither the Jewish nor the Christian division is totally logical. In the Tanak, the Writings remained open to the last of the books to enter the Hebrew Bible. The Tanak divides the

1

prophets into the earlier (which would include the story of Israel from Joshua to Kings) and the later (which comprises the prophetical works such as Isaiah, Jeremiah, Ezekiel, and the Twelve). The "Twelve" is the name traditionally used to designate the books of the twelve minor prophets, such as Hosea and Amos. These are the same in Christian and Jewish Bibles. Technically speaking, not all of the Twelve are in the prophetical genre (e.g., Jonah). In the Christian Bible, the division between poetical and prophetical is misleading. Most of the prophetical writings are expressed in poetry. There is a very complicated history behind the formation of the Bible, and the details of the divisions escape us. In general it can be argued that the Jewish division is the more significant one, in that it sets the Torah off in a class by itself, and this has left an unmistakable imprint on Judaism. In the case of the Christian division, the fourfold separation seems to be merely convenient, and governed by historical factors that escape us.

Q. 2. How else do Jewish and Christian Bibles differ?

In addition to the major fact that Christian Bibles have the New Testament, there are minor differences, such as the placing of the book of Daniel after Ezekiel (thus, four major prophets) in the Christian Bible. But the most significant difference exists between Catholic and Protestant Bibles. The Protestant Bible agrees with the Hebrew Bible. The Catholic Bible, however, has seven extra books and a few small parts (e.g., the prayer of Azariah and the Song of the three young men in Daniel 3). The Catholic surplus is known as the Deuterocanonical books (their canonical status was subject to doubt in past history), or the "apocrypha." These are now usually translated and often found in Bibles published under Protestant auspices (e.g., the *NRSV*), and they are identified explicitly as apocrypha. The tradition in the Orthodox churches of Christianity fluctuated, and even more books have been recognized as authoritative, such as 1 and 2 Esdras (contained in the *NRSV* edition with the apocrypha).

Fortunately, the chapter and verse numbering (a long-drawn-out process from the thirteenth to the sixteenth centuries) of the Old Testament books usually agrees in all the traditions. There are a few minor variations between Hebrew and Christian Bibles, but this is dependent upon chapter/verse divisions and is usually indicated in the translations. Thus, in many English versions, Malachi has four chapters (4:1–6 are 3:18–24 in the Jewish Bible). Perhaps the most confusing difference is to be found in the enumeration of verses in the book of Psalms. The current American Catholic translation (*NAB*) follows the Hebrew numbering, which includes the superscriptions or titles. But the usual English translation follows the British tradition and does not include these in the enumeration. Hence, the reader is often confronted with a difference of one or two digits (e.g., Ps 51:1 of *NRSV* is 51:3 in the numbering of the Hebrew Bible and the Catholic *NAB*, since these number the superscription as two lines).

Q. 3. How do these differences show up in the Writings?

First of all, the Writings include more books than do the so-called poetical books, as can be seen in the following lists:

Writings (Heb.)	*Poetical Books* (Prot.)	*Poetical Books* (Cath.)
Psalms	Job	Job
Job	Psalms	Psalms
Proverbs	Proverbs	Proverbs
Song of Songs	Ecclesiastes	Ecclesiastes
Ruth		
Ecclesiastes	Song of Songs	Song of Songs
	Plus:	Wisdom of Solomon
		Ecclesiasticus
Lamentations		
Esther		
Daniel		
Ezra-Nehemiah		
1–2 Chronicles		

The last five titles in the list of Writings are distributed differently in the Christian Bibles, but are all found there. The Catholic Bible, as mentioned above, has seven extra books, two of which are indicated in this list as germane to the wisdom literature of Israel (see Q. 20 below).

Q. 4. My Jewish friends often speak of the *megilloth* which are read on certain feasts. What are they?

The word *megilloth* means scrolls, and designates five books that came to be grouped together in the Writings: The Song of Songs, Ruth, Lamentations, Ecclesiastes, and Esther. The designation of the *megilloth* as a group did not occur until the early medieval period. The unity consists in the fact that they are read on particular religious feasts. Thus, Song of Songs for Passover; Ruth for Shavuoth, the feast of the grain harvest (Pentecost); Lamentations for the Ninth of Ab (anniversary of the destruction of Jerusalem); Ecclesiastes on the Sabbath of Succoth (Tabernacles); and Esther for the feast of Purim.

The term, "scroll," in itself designates a roll of material on which something is written. In antiquity papyrus and specially prepared leather served such purposes. They were rolled up for keeping and unrolled for reading. Early on, the codex or book form also appeared (e.g., the famous codex of the Greek Bible dating from the fourth century A.D.—the *Codex Vaticanus*). In their liturgical practice especially, the Jews have preserved the tradition of the scroll style.

PSALMS

Q. 5. Are the psalms prayers?

They are prayers, and more! They are called "praises" (*tehillim*) in the Jewish tradition. They are that, and more. Two very significant conclusions about the psalms have emerged in the past century of biblical scholarship. One is the liturgical character and background of the psalms and the other is their varied literary forms (such as hymns and laments). It is very helpful to approach the psalms with these two aspects in mind. They enable us to provide a probable life setting to the poems and to enter into their spirit. In a sense this is not a new insight. The ancients attempted to do something of this sort, but they were too specific. In the superscriptions or "titles" prefixed to psalms, David is indicated as author for seventy-three of them. It is impossible for us today to have any certainty concerning psalms that might have been written by David. As far as historical fact is concerned, the situation of authorship is similar to that of the wisdom books (Proverbs, Qoheleth) which were attributed to Solomon. In addition to David, several others are mentioned as "authors" (the word deserves to be put in quotation marks to indicate the loose association the psalm has to the putative authors): Asaph (Pss 74–82), Korah (42–49; 84–85; 87–88), and others.

The fact is that the titles are very ancient and we no longer understand the meaning of several words, perhaps liturgical directions, which appear in them: e.g., Psalm 22:1, "on the Deer of the Dawn"(?). These, like the mysterious *Selah* that appears within the psalms so many times, remain mysterious. We can overcome our ignorance, at least partially, by paying close attention to the literary forms and the implied liturgical settings.

Hymns. These are songs of praise, usually opened by the words of a leader urging a group to sing, exult, praise—all on a joyful note. The addressee is sometimes characterized as "the just" (Ps 33) or as the members of the heavenly court or "sons of God" (Ps 29 [see Q. 12 below]), or even as oneself (Ps 104). This opening is quickly followed by the enumeration of various things that evoke the praise. It is usually said that these are the "reasons" for the praise, since they are introduced by the Hebrew causal conjunction (*ki*). But the movement is not as rational as it sounds. The conjunction really serves to announce the marvels of the Lord in two general respects: God's creative activity (Ps 104), or the divine intervention in Israel's history (Ps 105). The beauty of this proclamation lies especially in the adroit repetition (secured by the phenomenon of poetic parallelism, in which two lines repeat or develop each other) and the lingering over events that are enumerated. There is a relish, a savoring, of the creative acts of God; creation is not "out of nothing," so much as it is God's loving continuation of the creative act—thus giving the addressee something to mull over and by which to be inspired. The hymns, especially, are characterized by singing and the use of musical instruments (Pss 147; 149–150).

Thanksgiving Songs. These are closely related to hymns, so much so that some scholars prefer to avoid the notion of thanksgiving, and speak instead of declarative praise. Thus, C. Westermann has pointed out that strictly speaking there is no word in Hebrew for "thanksgiving." Although the term appears in our English translation, it is really a translation of the word "praise" (*todah*). The point is well-taken. In our culture thanksgiving is an investment of one's person, and somewhat self-centered; it enables us to discharge a duty, the acknowledgment of a debt of some sort to another—in this case to God, for intervening in our lives. Whereas the spirit of these psalms is different: they leap to the acknowledgment of God who has acted as savior. The Lord has acted—praise be to God. It is important for us to realize the difference in point of view: God, not humans, is the focal point. Even though the psalmist goes on to relate the circumstances of the deliverance, the aim is to impress the bystanders, to give testimony to divine graciousness. A parade example of this type would be Psalm 30. It begins like a song of praise, but at once acknowledges the Lord as rescuer and urges the bystanders to learn from this experience: "Sing praise to the Lord, you faithful...divine favor lasts a life time." In many of these psalms there is also a flashback (30:7–11; 116:10–11), describing the prayer and the stressful situation to which the Lord responded. One can, however, still continue to use the term, "thanksgiving," to designate the particular form of this praise: it is in response to a personal rescue effected by the Lord, whereas the hymns generally are dealing with the momentous events of history and creation. The following can be classified as thanksgiving prayers of an individual: 10:1–13; 30; 32; 34; 40:2–11; 41; 66:13–20; 92; 116; 118; 138.

Laments. There are more laments than other types of prayer in the psalter: Psalms 3–7; 14 (=53); 17; 22; 25–28; 31; 35; 36; 38–39; 40:12–16; 42–43; 51; 54–57; 59; 61; 64; 69–71; 86; 88; 102; 130; 140–143. They reveal much about human beings and about God, even though the language seems extravagant to modern ears (e.g., the bulls, lions, dogs, sword, horns, that are afflicting the speaker in Psalm 22). Usually they begin with a cry for help, and go on to describe the suffering and distress that one wishes to be delivered from. The tone is lightened somewhat by the renewal of appeals to God, and the presentation of reasons why the Lord should intervene: because of the psalmist's trust (22:10–12), because of the covenant love that binds the Lord to the psalmist (thus in Psalm 89 the love and loyalty of the Lord are mentioned several times), or simply because of the trust that the psalmist has in God (13:6). In many psalms there is a remarkable turn in mood, as if the psalmist were already delivered (6:9–10; 22:23–32).

In addition to the laments of an individual, there are also laments of the community: 44:60; 74; 79; 80; 83; 85; 89; 90; 123. They resemble the laments of the individual in that certain motifs are common: Why has God allowed a setback to occur? Reasons why the Lord should intervene, and so forth. The prayers are often provoked by defeat in war: "Now you have rejected and disgraced us; you do not march out with our armies" (44:10). There is a boldness in language and freedom of spirit in the appeal to God: "Awake! Why do you sleep, O Lord? Rise up! Do not reject us forever!" (40:24).

The existence of laments within the Bible has a lesson for us—a lesson also indicated by the arguments of Job with God, or the "confessions" of Jeremiah (e.g., Jer 12:1–5). The ancient Israelite was at ease with God, even in adverse circumstances, and did not hesitate to question the Lord's ways. With typical directness, the question, "why?" dominates the laments. For various reasons the lament seems to have disappeared in modern prayer, especially among Christians. Perhaps it is present but unspoken. Or perhaps there is a mistaken notion that quarreling with God betrays a lack of faith, or a failure to recognize the divine will. Let us say, rather, that it is a way of discerning God's presence in the midst of difficulties, even of tragedy. Stoicism, or a "stiff upper lip," or constrained silence—these are not signs of virtue. The person of faith can freely voice cries for help and express the agony of suffering in the style of the psalmists.

The presence of the trust motif is a sign that the laments are not to be dismissed as mere complaints. The focus of the prayer is still God. Some are better described simply as psalms of trust: 11; 16; 23; 63; 91; 121; 125; 131; Psalms 91 and 121, especially, are examples of liturgical action in which a response from one of the Temple personnel assures the psalmist that trust is answered by divine protection: "God will not allow your foot to slip; your guardian does not sleep" (121:3). Are there any laments that seem to be sheerly desperate prayers? Perhaps Psalm 88, and also 39, would qualify. At the same time it should be noted that this "despair" is put in the form of a prayer; the desperate situation is commended to God. It has been remarked that in the psalter one can detect generally a movement from lament to praise. That is true in the sense that these are the two poles within which the moods of the psalmist fluctuate. The psalmist can never quite let go of God.

These literary types that I have described account for most of the prayers of the psalter. It can be seen that they have a simple structure, and depend on steady motifs that are frequently repeated. They capture the dominant moods of the psalmist and enable one to identify more easily with the movement in the psalm.

Q. 6. I have heard some psalms called "cursing psalms." What are they doing in the Bible?

Strictly speaking they are not a particular literary type. Cursing does occur in the psalms (especially the laments), and in many other books of the Bible. It is a fact of Old Testament life that should not be glossed over, and from which the modern Christian is not to be protected. I say this because many official publications of the psalter deliberately omit such disturbing lines, and are even authorized by liturgical directives to do so. Such censorship of the biblical text is misguided, to say the least. It is poor pedagogy, and a failure to confront reality.

Let us examine some of the possible reactions to the violence and vengeance of which we read in the scriptures. First, it does not make sense to be "scandalized" at a reality that is part of our own daily experience. Second, one should not react by sitting in judgment. Some would perhaps say, "this is not Christian," or the like. Of course! But who is the person who is not guilty of violent reactions, at least in his or her heart? It is self-serving to dismiss the violence of others as if it did not form part of our being and life. Third, we must *understand* the situation of Old Testament people. When injustice prevailed, where was God? Hence, they invoke divine punishment upon the wicked; they want to see justice done, and let the Lord look to it! We must also remember that justice was limited to *this* life, since beyond that there was only a shadowy existence in Sheol—neither reward nor punishment. Fourth, the language is vivid and seizes upon details to speak volumes. For example, many moderns state that they are shocked by the spectacle of Psalm 137:8, in which a blessing is pronounced over those who smash the babes of Babylon against a rock. When we examine the war and violence in our own culture, we have no right to be shocked, or to speak of the barbarity of the ancient world. Things have not changed, only words and means. We have "ethnic cleansing," starvation, atomic bombing; we are in no position to speak of the ancients as barbaric. Indeed the point of Psalm 137:8 is not so much the detail itself as the message of war, in which the slaughtering of the innocent usually occurs. The psalmist seizes upon a particularly gruesome detail, the accompaniment or aftermath of war, to represent the destruction of Babylon. The talion law is being applied: Babylon destroyed Jerusalem, now let Babylon be destroyed. We must remember that the talion law in itself was a means of establishing at least some equity in the conflicts of the ancient world: the punishment is not to exceed the crime.

I am not trying to exonerate the ancients. I am insisting that we moderns are not any better. It would be hypocritical of us to fail to see that any charge of barbarity must be levelled against ourselves as well. Still, one might claim that this is not a feature that is desirable in prayer: "When I pray I want to be at peace with all, and the Bible, especially the psalms, disturbs that mood." In other words, the difficulty seems to lie in the fact that these words of vengeance and violence are found on my lips, and I am directing them against others. Is there a way out of that? It depends upon how one articulates the psalm in question. It may be readily granted that it is not necessary to identify *with* the psalmist in such cases. One can easily identify with the psalmist when expressions of love, trust, loyalty, and so forth, are being expressed. But subjectively one may not be able to identify when the expressions are those of hatred (cf. e.g., Ps 139:19–24). What can be done? Instead of trying to identify, we can simply *hear* these words of violence. Hear them; do not dodge them. Let this vengeance become an accusation, an echo of the vengeance and hatred that lurks in our hearts. In that way such prayers remind us, and can even serve to accuse us of *our* failings. They are a mirror of the sinfulness of the world in which we all share, and they become a check on our own consciences and sinfulness. This reaction is much more realistic and salutary than closing one's eyes and ears to reality and, at least implicitly, thinking oneself as superior to one who cries out for vengeance. Such psalms become a healthy pointer to our own wrongdoing, and thus cannot be the occasion of self-congratulation. There is no room here for self-satisfaction.

Q. 7. Are there any other types of psalms that we should be aware of?

I described the main types in Q. 5 as praise, thanksgiving and lament, and I associated psalms of trust with the lament. There are also other ways of looking at the individual psalms—say, from the point of view of the subject matter. One can thus speak of Songs of Zion, Enthronement hymns, "liturgies," wisdom, and royal psalms. These designations derive from the content, rather than from the literary type. Among them are hymns, petitions, assurances of deliverance and thanksgiving.

Songs of Zion. These are songs of praise that deal with Jerusalem, seen as God's choice residence on earth: 46; 48; 76; 84; 87; 122; 132:11–18. Jerusalem is known as "the city of David," or Zion (2 Sam 5:7). It designates originally the stronghold of the Jebusites from whom David took over the city. David's move was more than political (choosing a neutral site in order to unify the various tribes). It was religious because he brought into Zion the Ark of the Covenant, and Zion became the religious capital, whose importance was sealed by the building of the Temple by Solomon (see the interpretation given in 1 Kings 8). The theology of the Temple is, in a sense, the theology of Zion. Here the Lord was thought to be invisibly enthroned on the Ark between the cherubim. The heavens could not contain God (1 Kgs 8:27), but in Zion the Lord chose also to dwell (Ps 132). In the view of Deuteronomy, this could be expressed by saying that the divine Name was here. That was the manner of God's presence. The presence of God remains a theological mystery for us today, and one can see how Israel struggled with it. In the view of the Priestly tradition, it was said that the Lord "pitched tent" in Jerusalem. This notion continues from the Old Testament into the New Testament where it is picked up by John 1:14 (this refers literally to the Word pitching a tent), and one expression for the presence of God in Jewish tradition is derived from this notion (the Shekinah). It is not surprising, then, that Zion should become a focal point of Israel's praise. It is "the holy mountain," "the joy of all the earth" (Ps 48:2–3); "God is in its midst; it shall not be shaken" (46:6); "The Lord loves the city founded on holy mountains" (87:1).

Enthronement psalms. These commemorate the kingship of the Lord: 47; 93; 97–99. The characteristic cry is: "The Lord is king!" (97:1; 99:1). Jubilant cries greeted the Jerusalemite king, when he ascended the throne (cf. 2 Kgs 9:13), and these were transposed to the cult where the Lord's kingship was celebrated. The divine reign was anchored in the work of creation and its maintenance and also in rule and judgment over the whole world. Was there a specific feast of

Enthronement of yhwh? S. Mowinckel (*The Psalms in Israel's Worship* [New York: Abingdon, 1962]) argued for its existence and he included several more psalms in this category. He may have exaggerated, but the celebration of the Lord's kingship is certainly the spirit of these psalms.

Liturgies. In a sense most of the psalms are liturgies of one sort or another, since they were generally composed for cultic use. But "liturgies" is used here to designate those prayers that illustrate some specific kind of liturgical action. For example, Psalms 15 and 24 exemplify question and response as one would enter the Temple: "Who may dwell on your holy mountain?" (15:1). The question tests the worthiness of one who would approach the holy place: who would dare? The response is "whoever walks without blame...." Antiphonal singing is illustrated by Psalm 136 with the refrain, "God's love endures forever." And in many instances one can see that the psalmist is a kind of master of ceremonies giving directions, for example, in 33:1–3; 34:4; 134; 135:1–4.

Wisdom psalms. There is no general agreement on the exact criteria for determining a wisdom psalm, and hence there is no unanimity concerning the number of these poems. All would probably agree that the alphabetic acrostic, Psalm 37, can be so classified because it consists of sayings that are in the style of those contained in the book of Proverbs, e.g., "Better the poverty of the just than the great wealth of the wicked. The arms of the wicked will be broken; the Lord will sustain the just" (37:16–17). In lieu of the absence of criteria it is more satisfactory to speak of wisdom influence on certain psalms, as in 34:12, "Come, children, listen to me; I will teach you the fear of the Lord." For further details, see R. E. Murphy, *The Tree of Life* (New York: Doubleday, 1990) 97–110.

Royal psalms. These have to do with the currently reigning king, and are thus classified by reason of content. In terms of literary type, they can be petitions (20) or thanksgiving (21) or even a poem on the occasion of a royal marriage (45). The following are generally considered as royal psalms: 2; 18 (cf. 144:1–11); 20; 21; 45; 72; 101; and 110. It is perhaps difficult for the modern reader to enter into the spirit of these poems. They seem to be merely antiquarian in interest, since they refer literally to the currently reigning king. But the question can be asked: why were these royal psalms preserved after the destruction of Jerusalem and the end of the royal Davidic line in 597? I will consider this in the discussion of messianism (see Q. 13).

Q. 8. Can you offer any help to those who find it hard to pray the psalms?

Let me begin with a negative statement: one cannot pray what one does not understand. In other words, an understanding of the literary types and liturgical character of the psalms aids us to get into the spirit of a given psalm and thus to determine its prayer value for us. The previous discussion bears on this point. Moreover, it is not necesssary for us to like all the psalms. Some more than others become favorites: one thinks of Psalm 23 ("The Lord is my shepherd") or 51 ("Have mercy on me...") and others that have achieved widespread acceptance. There are many more that call for our attention, if only we confront them and analyze them.

I do not mean that a knowledge of the types and liturgical background is the only answer to your question. It is also necessary to understand the worldview of the psalmist. We present aspects of this below in Q. 12. Let us consider one point as an example, the notion of Sheol, or the nether world.

At first sight it would seem that the absence of a belief in a future life with God would present an insuperable difficulty for Christian prayer. Belief in a future life seems so central to Christian self-understanding. But two factors render this absence less of a problem. First of all, the Christian has to admire the faith of the Israelites. They took God on God's terms: Sheol is the fate of all, good and evil alike. Many Christians tend to use personal eschatology as a crutch; but the idea of reward/punishment should not be allowed to dominate the outlook of faith. Appropriating the Old Testament view can purify the faith of an over-eschatologized Christian. They lived with God in the present, and so must we even if we have a belief in a future life. It is the present that decides the future.

Second, the Old Testament expressions about "life," "salvation," and other key realities remain open to further interpretation according to the perspective of the reader. We do not have to limit ourselves to the biblical views. We can expand them in the light of later revelation.

But it is important to begin with the Old Testament in order to appreciate the eschatological dimension that can be given to it. One might say that the biblical concepts are infinitely expandable in the light of God's designs. Many scholars have pointed out the paradox here. Although the psalms directly relate to this life as a rule, they have brought steady comfort to the dying who are looking forward to a better life. Dietrich Bonhoeffer captured the spirit of this fact by insisting on the need for the Old Testament. He wrote from prison that it was "not Christian to want to take our thoughts and feelings too quickly and too directly from the New Testament" (*Letters and Papers from Prison* [rev. ed., New York: Macmillan, 1967] 86). He continues in the same vein with the practical observations: "My thoughts and feelings seem to be getting more and more like those of the Old Testament, and in recent months I have been reading the Old Testament much more than the New. It is only when one knows the unutterability of the name of God that one can utter the name of Jesus Christ; it is only when one loves life and the earth so much that without them everything seems to be over that one can believe in the resurrection and a new world." These statements are extravagant but on target. They tell us that Christians must go through the Old Testament to the New if they are to assess correctly their own identity. A reverence for the sacred Name, *yhwh*, undergirds belief in Jesus Christ; the goodness of creation has to be affirmed along with the newness that is to come.

Third, it is necessary to grasp the notion of Sheol as a *dynamic power* which manifests itself in this life. One could call this a metaphorical use of Sheol, but some might think, just a metaphor? No, it stands for things that are quite real: sickness, opposition, personal unhappiness and failure, enemies. In other words, all the obstacles one faces in daily life—these are manifestations of Sheol; one is in the "hand" or power of Sheol (e.g., Ps 89:49). In a word, Sheol means non-life; it is not accidental that it is so often in parallelism with death; they are genuine word-pairs. To the extent that we experience non-life, to that extent we are in Sheol. This is a profound insight into reality: Death exercises a dominion over us long before we die. We may not trivialize this in terms of the aging process about which we can do nothing. No, Sheol stands for what beleaguers us, overwhelms us. Now we can understand the triumphant cry of thanksgiving in Psalm 30:4, "O Lord, you brought me up from Sheol." This is not resuscitation or resurrection, but deliverance from some manifestation of non-life in the here and now.

This is only one example of the worldview that suffuses the psalms and the entire Old Testament. We must acquire a certain familiarity with these categories. See Q. 12.

Q. 9. But aren't you saying that I must pray the psalms as an Old Testament believer? I want to pray them as a Christian!

I think I am saying that one should pray the psalms with an understanding of what the psalmist meant to say. That's all, but it is important. It is a *beginning* which leads to praying them "as a Christian." The experience of the psalmist, both joys and sorrows, are terribly human, and it is on this level that we are affected in life. We must meet these circumstances, often terrifying, with faith, and the faith manifested in the psalms can inspire us to perseverance and steadfastness. This is a very realistic way of praying the psalms, and one may claim that this would have been the way followed by Jesus and his followers. You will recall that Psalm 22, a song of desolation (as well as of ultimate victory) is on the lips of Jesus, according to Matthew 27:46 (cf. also Mk 15:34). This is in agreement with the striking words of the letter to the Hebrews 5:7, "Jesus offered up prayers and supplications, with loud cries and tears, to the one who was able to save him from death...."

However, your question deserves a fuller answer than I have given. You may wish to pray the psalms in a Christocentric way, with Christ the focus of these prayers. This approach can be reconciled with what I have been saying. Thus, the experience of the one who suffers in Psalm 22 can be seen and interpreted on the level of the sufferings of Christ. One can invoke the time-honored practice of Christian typology: that the Old Testament psalmist is a type of Christ in his sufferings. Or one can simply expand the interpretive level of Psalm 22 and recognize in the suffering psalmist the One who suffered most of all, and for the sake of all. You see, there are many levels at which we can prolong the psalms into our own Christian experience. We can meditate upon them as reflecting the sufferings of ourselves, of Jesus, or of the martyrs. See also QQ. 10, 13.

My concern has been to keep us from neglecting the power of the literal historical meaning of the psalms, and its application to ourselves. I grant that there are many ways in which we can prolong or continue the psalms into our Christian experience. It is just that I do not want to see the Old Testament flattened out into one level, Jesus and me. After all, Jesus sang the hymns to the Lord, *yhwh*, who is the God and Father whom he called "Abba."

Q. 10. What do you mean when you say we can pray the psalms in a Christocentric way?

By that I mean a reading of the Old Testament in such a way that one refers everything explicitly to Christ and the events of his life. It is an attitude to the Old Testament that manifests itself in several different approaches. The attitude emphasizes the preparatory character of the Old Testament in such a way that its value lies in its orientation to the future, to the fulfillment in Christ. One approach is strict prediction, which is perhaps best illustrated in the history of the interpretation of the so-called messianic psalms (on this see Q. 13). Another is the typological approach mentioned in Q. 9, i.e., an Old Testament person or event becomes a type or figure of a person or event in the New Testament. There is a correspondence between the divine activity in the Testaments. This typological mindset is genuinely biblical, and can be seen within the Old Testament itself, as when the Exodus deliverance becomes a type of the deliverance of Israel from Babylon (cf. e.g., Isa 41:17–20; 43:16–21). Similarly, St. Paul regards Adam as a type of Jesus Christ in Romans 5. The letter to the Hebrews makes several connections between Old and New; see the treatment of Abraham in Hebrews 11:8–19. I do not deny that the typological approach is valid. My practical judgment is that it does not appeal to modern readers; the power of typological symbolism is lost for most of them.

The Christocentrism of St. Augustine lies more in the mood of the one who prays than in the words of the psalm. This mood can be perceived in the remarks of his commentary on Psalm 85: Jesus Christ, son of God, "prays for us and prays in us and is prayed to us, as our God. Let us recognize, therefore, our words in him, and his words in us.... Therefore we pray to him, through him; we speak with him and he speaks with us." Because there are no real laws for prayer style, we are perfectly free to pray in this vein. It may not be the style for everyone. The association with Christ is more an ambience than a meaning inherent in the psalm.

Q. 11. Is there a connection between poetry and prayer?

Yes, very definitely, and I want to indicate this by quotations from a theologian and a poet. The theologian is the late Karl Rahner, S.J. In an essay on "Poetry and the Christian" (*More Recent Writings* [Theological Investigations IV; Baltimore: Helicon, 1966] 357–67), he takes up the question of understanding the Bible, the word of God in general, so much of which is expressed in poetic lines in the Old Testament: "And so it is true that the capacity and the practice of perceiving the poetic word is a presupposition of hearing the word of God...the poetic word and the poetic ear are so much part of man that if this essential power were really lost to the heart, man could no longer hear the word of God in the word of man. In its inmost essence, the poetic is a prerequisite for Christianity" (p. 363).

The poet is Thomas Merton (*Bread in the Wilderness* [New York: New Directions, 1953] 53):

"The psalms are poems, and poems have a meaning—although the poet has no obligation to make his meaning immediately clear to anyone who does not want to make an effort to discover it. But to say that poems have meaning is not to say that they must necessarily convey practical information or an explicit message. In poetry, words are charged with meaning in a far different way than are the words in a piece of scientific prose. The words of a poem are not merely the signs of concepts: they are also rich in affective and spiritual associations. The poet uses words not merely to make declarations, statements of fact. That is usually the last thing that concerns him. He seeks above all to put words together in such a way that they exercise a mysterious and vital reactivity among themselves, and so release their secret content of associations to produce in the reader an experience that enriches the depths of his spirit in a manner quite unique. A good poem induces an experience that could not be produced by any other combination of words. It is therefore an entity that stands by itself, graced with an individuality that marks it off from every other work of art. Like all great works of art, true poems seem to live by a life entirely their own. What we must seek in a poem is therefore not an accidental reference to something outside itself: we must seek this inner principle of individuality and of life which is its soul, or "form." What the poem actually "means" can only be summed up in the whole content of poetic experience which it is capable of producing in the reader. This total poetic experience is what the poet is trying to communicate to the rest of the world. It is supremely important for those who read the Psalms and chant them in the public prayer of the Church to grasp, if they can, the poetic content of these great songs.... [This] does mean that the type of reader whose poetic appetites are fully satisfied by the Burma Shave rhymes along our American highways may find it rather hard to get anything out of the Psalms.

Both Rahner and Merton are pointing to the latent poetic faculties that exist in every human being. They are not saying that *we* can write poetry, but only that we can and must react to poetic symbol if we are to appreciate the biblical passage that is cast in poetic form.

These words of Rahner and Merton deserve study and meditation on our part. Rahner says that we are ultimately poetic in that we have the ability to react to imagery. Hence, our need to pay attention to this imagery and learn to savor it (Zion, Sheol, Leviathan, and so forth). This we probably have to learn, at least at the beginning, but our own poetic imagination develops along with it. Merton points out the associations that go with certain poetic concepts and expressions. These beget an experience in a manner that a flat statement of fact does not. The latter can leave us cold. We can possibly be moved by depth of emotion, the outcry, the anger, the adoration—in short, by the vivid humanness that is reflected in so many of the various types of psalms. This poetic touch may not come to us immediately; we may have to relish and not rush over certain poems. Perhaps a few examples will highlight this. How would a reporter describe the relationship of shepherd and sheep as related in Psalm 23? How would a TV commentator relate the failure of expectations expressed in Psalm 89? How would a professor of science portray the sense of nearness to the creator that the psalmist professes in Psalm 139? Finally, how do you react to these psalms?

Q. 12. You have mentioned the Israelite "worldview." Why is knowing their view of the world important for understanding the psalms?

Indeed there are many other examples, and it is appropriate to consider them here. Since the psalms were written over a period of some seven centuries, they furnish a cross section of Israelite thought. The presuppositions of the average modern reader often need to be changed in the light of Israel's understanding of reality. At this point let us limit ourselves to four examples.

The first is the word, "soul," which we tend to interpret in the light of later theology as a spiritual, immortal, substantial part of a human being. This is not the biblical view, even if "soul" appears in English translation. We don't have adequate terms to translate words like *nephesh* (life force), *neshamah* (life breath) and *ruah* (wind, spirit). Hence "soul" is used in lieu of a better term. So in Psalms 103, 104, the psalmist is speaking to self, not to the soul as we understand it. The description of creation in Genesis 2:7 gives us the key to what a human being is: breathed-upon matter, not body/soul. God breathed the "breath of life" into the nostrils of the man formed from the ground, and the man was a living being. In Psalm 104:30 creation is ascribed to God's spirit which is sent forth and the face of the earth is renewed.

Second, there is the inexact use of the word, monotheism, to describe biblical belief. Monotheism must be understood as a belief which developed over many centuries. If we define it as the existence of only one God, thus excluding the existence of other divinities, it appears only in the post-exilic period, helped by the great theological insights in Isaiah 40–55. Israelite belief before this time is better described as henotheism, that is, one God among many: "The Lord is the great God, the great king over all gods" (Ps 95:3; cf. 97:7–9). The Lord is God, but other divinities exist. As Deuteronomy 32:8 describes the situation,

When the Most High assigned the nations their heritage,
when he parceled out the descendants of Adam,

> He set up the boundaries of the peoples
> after the number of the sons of God. (*NAB*)

In the psalter there is a constant cry: who is like to you among the gods? (86:8; 89:7–9). Of course, there is no one; the Lord is incomparable. But God is pictured as the head of a group who are called the "sons of El" or sons of God (so, literally, the translation of Ps 29:1). In the course of time lesser divinities are seen to be the servants who carry out the Lord's commands (e.g., the sons of Elohim in Job 1:6), who are "sent" by God (and hence called "angels"). Israel's profession of faith is described in Deuteronomy 6:4, "Hear, O Israel! The Lord is our God, the Lord alone!" This short description of biblical "monotheism" might seem to be unnecessary, but it is not. For it gives historical depth to a theological abstraction (monotheism), and it makes one appreciate the significance of monotheistic belief. It also affects the interpretation of such psalms as 58 and 82.

Third, there is a close association between sin and suffering. The general understanding is that suffering of any kind has been brought about by one's wrongdoing, or by the sin of the parents or community (cf. Jn 9:2). Someone had to bear the responsibility! And of course, if there was no consciousness of personal wrongdoing, the problem of divine responsibility usually arose (cf. the book of Job). In the laments of the psalter God is frequently described as angry and as the agent of suffering: "Do not reprove me in your anger, Lord, nor punish me in your wrath" (Ps 6:2). Even when one is aware of personal sinfulness, the psalmist tries to assuage the divine wrath: "My flesh is afflicted because of your anger; my frame aches because of my sin" (Ps 38:4). These accusations may flow in some cases from a desire to move God to intervene, to bring the Lord to heel, since the punishment is more than the psalmist deserves. It is another example of realism. The psalmist refuses, as it were, to believe that the Lord could go to such extremes in punishment; let God get over the fit of anger that is motivating this trouble.

One must also be prepared for the puzzling ways in which righteousness and sinfulness figure in the psalms. In general, the Old Testament is quite free in the portrayal of human sinfulness, especially in the psalms (e.g., 51). But one can be brought up short before such prayers as Psalm 26:

> Grant me justice, Lord!
>   I have walked without blame...
> I will wash my hands in innocence
>   and walk around your altar, Lord...
> Do not take me away with sinners....
> I walk without blame....

Here the psalmist puts forth personal righteousness (even if humanity is sinful!) as the principal argument of the prayer. That is the reason God should intervene: "Do not take me away with sinners...." This is not an examination of conscience; it is a declaration of loyalty (see also Ps 139:19–24), a statement concerning the psalmist's better self. The psalmist is even aware that there must be a test:

> Test me, Lord, and try me;
>   search my heart and mind.
> Your love is before my eyes;
>   I walk guided by your faithfulness (26:2–3).

All this implies an understanding of divine activity which still remains very mysterious. The assumption is that the Lord is the cause of both good and evil. This is asserted at various times in the Bible (Isa 45:7; Amos 3:6). The direct agency of the Lord made suffering all the more excruciating. What did it say about one's relationship to God? One partial and paradoxical answer was given in the admonition of Proverbs 3:11–12: Do not spurn the Lord's reproof because this is a sign of divine love—a recommendation taken up in the letter to the Hebrews 12:5–6! One could also interpret various trials as a "testing," as when it is explicitly said that God put Abraham to the test (Gen 22:1). The book of Job shows that Israel constantly grappled with this problem, without ever coming to a definitive answer. The writer of Psalm 37 advises that one should not be envious of the wicked—they will get their comeuppance. But the writer of Psalm 73 describes the agony that injustice creates, almost to the destruction of faith. In the psalms there is a lively dialogue concerning this problem.

Fourth, the idea of creation in the psalms is strikingly different from the majestic description of the six-day creation by divine word in

Genesis 1. Creation is now described as conflict—conflict with monsters that personify the power of chaos:

> You stirred up the Sea in your might;
> you smashed the heads of the dragons on the waters.
> You crushed the heads of Leviathan,
> tossed him for food to the sharks.
> You opened up spring and torrents,
> brought dry land out of the primeval waters (Ps 74:13–15).

This expression of the creative power of the Lord borrows from the cultural world in which Israel lived, the creation stories of Mesopotamia, and the battles between Baal and Yam (Sea) detailed for us in the Ugaritic literature. We recognize here the creative imagination of the Israelite poets who stand in vivid contrast to the abstractions of modern theology; see also Psalms 89:10–11; 114; Isaiah 51:9–10; Habakkuk 3:8–10.

Other aspects of the biblical worldview will surface in the other books of the Writings that we will be discussing.

Q. 13. I thought there were messianic psalms; why haven't you mentioned them?

I have spoken of royal psalms in Q. 7 and there I hinted at messianic psalms, but I think it better to separate the two ideas. We must first agree on the definition of messiah. From the etymological point of view that is easy. Messiah means anointed. Who are anointed in ancient Israel? The king, not the priest (except in the post-exilic period). Although we usually associate the latter with anointing, it is clear that the king was the anointed par excellence. The most striking example is David's conduct. When he has an opportunity to remove his enemy, King Saul, he only cuts off the edges of Saul's cloak. But even this troubles him: Why? Because Saul is the Lord's anointed (1 Sam 24:1–7). The king is a sacral figure.

Throughout the ancient Near East kingship was regarded highly, and in Egypt the Pharaoh was even divinized. There is a striking contrast when one considers how the Israelite prophets attacked reigning kings and the power structure. They did this in the name of the Lord and for the sake of righteousness. Along with this, however, a certain aura attached to the Davidic descendants. David had received assurance from the Lord through the prophet Nathan that there would always be one of his descendants reigning in Jerusalem (2 Sam 7:11–17). This transformed the kingship, and there is constant reference to reigning kings in the light of the promise to David. This royal messianism is developed at length by several prophets, preeminently Isaiah, and it is manifest in the proud claims made for the reigning kings in the royal psalms (see Q. 7 above). With the Lord to ensure the Davidic line, a great future was assured. We should emphasize that this messianic promise is dynastic; it attaches to the descendants of David as a whole, and not to one individual as *the* messiah.

What happened to this promise? The Davidic dynasty was eliminated with the fall of Jerusalem in 587 to the Babylonians, and Israel became a captive people. The agony and perplexity of this event are rehearsed in Psalm 89. The psalmist begins by celebrating the Lord's love and fidelity to his promises (and repeats these words continually through the psalm!). Then the promise to David is singled out:

> Forever I will maintain my love for him;
>   my covenant with him stands firm.
> I will establish his dynasty forever,
>   his throne as the days of the heavens....
> By my holiness I swore once for all:
>   I will never be false to David.
> His dynasty will continue forever... (89:29–37).

The tune changes and the Lord is charged with having gone back on his word. It is likely that this psalm comes from the days of the fall of Jerusalem; if it referred to an earlier calamity it was far more true of those days:

> Where are your promises of old, Lord,
>   the loyalty sworn to David? (89:50)

Despite Israel's continued subjection to the foreign powers of Persia and the Greeks, the hope in the Davidic dynasty never died out. In fact, if there were ever a time to discard the royal psalms, it would have been now, from the sixth century onward. Instead, the royal psalms were preserved. Why? What sense did they make? No sense at all, unless they were reinterpreted. The unknown prophet of the Exile had proclaimed that the word of God stands forever (Isa 40:8). The hope in a future David, a David *redivivus*, never disappeared. The glories of the old kingdom were nourished in many quarters, and the promise of a dynasty became centered on one who would surely come. In the days of Christ, this Anointed One was understood to be a warrior, like David. Surely he would lift the yoke of Rome from the shoulders of God's people!

But it is obvious that the messiahship that Christ had in mind did not share in those dreams. Indeed, they were an obstacle to Jesus in his ministry. He refused to be cast in that mold, and he had to transform the notion of messiah (Son of Man, Suffering Servant). When we examine the New Testament, we find royal messianism appearing mainly in the infancy narratives of Matthew and Luke, which are later compositions that came from the church reflecting on the risen Christ. On this see also J. A. Fitzmyer, S. J., *A Christological Catechism: New Testament Answers* (2d ed.; New York: Paulist, 1991) 62–66; 102–8.

There is an interesting parallel between Jews and Christians in this respect. The Jews before the time of Christ read the royal psalms as having a future. The Christians regard that future as past, fulfilled in Christ. Hence, the Christians also reinterpret the royal psalms, but as testifying to the coming of Jesus the Christ. They are not predictions of future events relative to Christ; they refer historically to the reigning king for whom they were written. Then they received a thrust to the future, and became a source of hope during dire centuries. When the Christ came he played down messianism, transforming the future figure according to his own ideals. Christians tend to forget that they *believe* that Jesus is the messiah. It is not a conclusion from reason; it may be reasonable to believe, but it is not susceptible to logical proof. The use of the royal psalms in Christian prayer represents a long loving look backward to the origins of the Christ among the people of God. We can learn much from Peter at Caesarea Philippi. Mark 8:29–33 describes how Peter acknowledges that Jesus is the messiah, and how the Lord forbids his closest disciples to spread this about (8:30–31), that the Son of man must suffer. When Peter challenges this, Jesus delivers the astonishing words: "Get behind me, Satan! For you are thinking not as God does, but as human beings do."

Q. 14. You approach the psalms individually according to types. But is it possible to interpret the psalms as a book, as a whole?

I see your point. You can argue that after all we don't break down other biblical books into chapters and study these alone without regard to context. I have been putting the psalms in a literary and liturgical context. You are asking whether there is a "book" context. Does a psalm acquire another meaning when it becomes scripture, finally entering into a collection?

1. First, there is the immediate context of a psalm to be considered. Several psalms may be grouped together on the basis of catchwords, and these catchwords serve to give a nuance to a poem. It doesn't change a hymn into a complaint, but it gives a coloring to a psalm that should not be neglected. G. Wilson (*The Editing of the Hebrew Psalter* [Chico: Scholars Press, 1985] 193–4) has illustrated the movement that exists between the various Hallelujah psalms in 146–50. The last verse of Psalm 145 (a psalm of David!) proclaims praise of God from "my mouth" and from "all flesh." This is taken up by the psalmist in 146:2—a praise of a whole lifetime. The movement continues: in Psalm 147 the dispersed of Israel (v 2) are "gathered" and Zion is commanded to praise God. In Psalm 148 this chorus of praise is expanded to the heavens above (angels, sun and moon, etc.) and to the cosmos below (sea monsters, deep waters, mountains, hills, animals). The reason is that the Lord "has lifted high the horn of his people" (148:14). Hence, in Psalm 149:1 there is a "new song" of praise from the "faithful." Then finally in Psalm 150, to the accompaniment of the whole orchestra, "everything that has breath" is to give praise to the Lord. So there is kind of inclusio from Psalm 145:21, "all flesh," to 150:6, "all that breathes." Within this there is a movement, as *all* of creation is spelled out and united in a high paean of praise to God. Unless one treats the context of these poems, one will miss the higher unity and message that is implied by their grouping. We glide from one psalm to another, embracing several levels of meaning. While praise of the Lord

is the common denominator, we feel a strong pull to identify with the various parts of creation and community in this chorus of praise.

Second, Psalm 1 has been singled out as saying more than it does, when its position as the introductory psalm is considered. Considered by itself, it is unusual within the psalter. There are not many beatitudes (cf. Ps 32). This is a beatitude that sharply divides the righteous from sinners, and their separate ways are described. The prime activity of the righteous is meditating (this was an oral, not mental, recitation) on the law of the Lord who watches over the way of the just. In contrast, the way of the wicked perishes. There is hardly a more central topic than this for the entire Bible, much less for the psalms. What will be the choice? For God or not? As an introduction, Psalm 1 sets up a standard for personal piety, an orientation to the divine will expressed in the Torah. There is nothing here of liturgy, although we have postulated liturgical origins for so many psalms. Rather, the psalms have come to be read as Torah, or instruction (the basic meaning of this word) for the pious faithful concerning the two ways.

One can also take a cue from the verb in Psalm 1:3, "meditate," or "study." This does not mean silent contemplation of the text; it means audible recitation. In the ancient world there were few texts available to be read or contemplated. One knew the key passages by heart and recited them. Thus, the command is given in Deuteronomy 6:6–7: "Take to heart these words which I enjoin on you today. Drill them into your children. Speak of them at home and abroad, whether you are busy or at rest." They didn't carry a Bible around with them. They knew these words by heart, and they recited them. The psalter is a "meditation" book in the sense that it becomes, day and night, the object of recitation and study. In other words, these prayers which were originally addressed *to* God can be seen as teaching addressed *from* God to the faithful.

We have already noted the paradoxical fact that the liturgical origins postulated for so many psalms are nowhere indicated for the pre-exilic period, i.e., there is nothing in the liturgical instructions in the Torah which bears on the use of the psalms. There are only a few references to music and singing in Chronicles, and these may reflect a late practice, although describing the dedication of Solomon's Temple (2 Chron 5:12–14; cf. 7:6). A pastiche of psalms (105:1–15; 96:1–13 and 106:1,47–48) is recorded in 1 Chronicles 16, where David installs the

Ark of the Covenant. Hence, we have no first-hand evidence of the liturgical use of the psalms, although the psalter has been traditionally and perhaps mistakenly called "the prayer book of the Second Temple."

We have two indications that the psalms were very popular. One indication is the presence of evidence for some thirty copies in the caves of Qumran. It should be remembered, however, that the Jews in Qumran wrote their own compositions, such as the *Hodayot* ("thanksgiving psalms"), and the style was "anthological composition," i.e., a composition formed mainly out of biblical phraseology.

The import of these considerations is considerable. First, we are witnessing a change in the interpretation of the Bible *within* the Bible itself. This inner-biblical development is not new; it has been noted for other books of the Bible as well. Second, the development is not to be considered as a binding interpretation, as though the only way to approach the psalms must now be as an object of study, an instruction. That is one way, and a fruitful way. Third, we are already launched into the history of the changing role of the Bible, and specifically the psalms. We do not have the historical sources to sketch out such a history for both Judaism and Christianity. It may be said that for most of the period in which the Talmud was written, little use of the psalms was made in Jewish liturgy. The major emphasis was on the Torah. Christians continued their interest in the psalms, already evidenced by the frequent quotations and allusions to them within the New Testament. The predictive aspects of the so-called messianic psalms were emphasized in apologetics. But the real impetus to the psalms came from monasticism, both in the East and West. The psalter became the prayerbook of the monks, and this filtered down to the laity as well.

Q. 15. Are there any psalms in the Bible found outside of the book of Psalms?

Yes, there are several. One of the most interesting cases, from the textual point of view, is Psalm 18 which matches 2 Samuel 22:2–51. The two poems seem to be doublets. The superscription is practically the same as 2 Samuel 22:1, so the setting is one of thanksgiving for having been delivered from enemies by the Lord. Noteworthy are the mythological traits of a theophany as the Lord thunders, shoots arrows, and delivers the psalmist from the abyss. The Lord does this only for the righteous, and the psalmist is not embarrassed to underscore this (18:21–31). The poem ends on the note of assurance for the Davidic dynasty (2 Sam 22:51=Ps 18:51). In this respect it is similar to another psalm which opens the books of Samuel, the Canticle of Hannah in 1 Samuel 2:1–10. It is Hannah's response to the Lord for the birth of her son, Samuel, and its similarity to the Magnificat of Mary (Luke 1:46–55, another "psalm," by the way) has often been noted. But this psalm is probably originally a victory hymn, a song of thanksgiving to the Lord for having delivered the people and the king (cf. 1 Sam 2:10). Thus, the books of Samuel open and close with psalms, in these two cases for "the anointed." And in 2 Samuel 23:1–7 a short psalm has been introduced under the guise of being "the last words of David" and it refers (v 5) to the "everlasting covenant with David." The tradition of "last words" and blessings from a patriarch is an old one in Israel (cf. Gen 49:1; Deut 33:1; these poems, too, are psalms).

Anyone who has paid attention to the various literary types in the psalter will be alert to these genres when they appear in other books. Several psalms appear among the books of the prophets, such as Isaiah 12. Here are two songs of "thanksgiving" or praise, both with prose introductions, "you shall say on that day" (vv 1,4). In Isaiah 63:7–64:12 is a beautiful supplication in which the poet intercedes with the Lord ("our father") to intervene in favor of his people. Among the apocrypha, perhaps the most famous is a wisdom poem, in autobiographical style, in which Ben Sira describes his love for pursuit of Wisdom and invites all to seek her out (Sir 51:13–30). It has become famous because several verses of this acrostic poem were found in the eleventh cave of Qumran, along with some noncanonical psalms. A typical psalm of thanksgiving is also found in Sirach 51:1–12). More wisdom poems appear in Proverbs 1–9.

Q. 16. What are the shortest, and the longest psalms?

The shortest psalm is 117. So short is it, in fact, that we may as well record it here:

> Praise the Lord, all you nations!
> Give glory, all you peoples!

The Lord's love for us is strong;
the Lord is faithful forever.
Hallelujah!

These two verses call for some comment. Note, first of all, that the genre is a hymn of praise, and the command is addressed to the gentiles, no less. One could say that the psalmist invokes all the living to praise the Lord, but it still remains worthy of note that the gentiles are specifically mentioned. Verse 2 may be simply an affirmation of the Lord's worldwide rule, but it indicates a reason personal to Israel: the Lord's covenant love and fidelity (the keeping of the promises to the people). The summons to the nations is found also in other psalms, such as 22:28–29; 100:1.

The longest psalm is 119, and it is quite unique. One should not be put off by its unusual acrostic character. There are 22 strophes, each of 8 verses, corresponding to the number of letters in the Hebrew alphabet, and each verse in a strophe begins with the same letter of the alphabet—thus, an *aleph* strophe, followed by a *beth* strophe, etc. Furthermore, with the exception of one verse, each of the 176 verses has some sort of synonym for *torah* (law, teaching) in it, such as word, decree, edict, etc. All this might suggest that the poem is rigid and unappealing. Not so. The dominant note is the will of the Lord for the worshipper. And what are the various attitudes of the worshipper to God's will? Obedience, love, delight, praise, desire, hope, and so forth. The wide range of views concerning the Torah of God is remarkable. It is a psalm detailing the revelation of God and human response. One should not be deceived by the frequent mention of law and commands. This is a hymn of delight and submission to God.

PROVERBS

Q. 17. What is a proverb?

Perhaps the most famous answer to this question was given by Archer Taylor (*The Proverb and an Index to the Proverb* [2nd ed.; Copenhagen and Hatboro: Rosenkilde & Baggers, 1962] 3): "The definition of a proverb is too difficult to repay the undertaking.... An incommunicable quality tells us this sentence is proverbial and that one is not.... Let us be content with recognizing that a proverb is a saying current among the folk." We cannot be satisfied with that, except for Archer's emphasis on currency. Presumably several of the biblical proverbs survived because they gained currency, but it is equally possible that others, such as the great number that deal with the righteous and wicked may not have enjoyed that circulation. Those are all terribly uniform, and they overwhelm by reason of their number rather than by clever expression. What was popular in one social group may not have caught on with another. We are not helped by the Hebrew word *mashal*, which is applied too widely in the Bible to be of help. The meaning of the root is twofold: "rule" (and hence the power of the word?) and "comparison" (admittedly there are many pungent comparisons among the biblical proverbs).

If definition is difficult or even impossible, identification is much easier. Just read the book of Proverbs from chapter 10 on. In the main we are confronted with two line sayings that reflect on human conduct, and they are expressed in some form of parallelism (A, and even more so, B). Commands and admonitions are also included and some example stories that one can compare to New Testament parables. There is also what may be called the wisdom poem, found in Proverbs 1–9.

What I have said would hardly tempt you to pick up the book of Proverbs with eagerness and anticipation. The description of J. G. Williams ("The Power of Form: A Study of Biblical Proverbs," in *Gnomic Wisdom* [Semeia 17; ed. J. D. Crossan; Chico: Scholars Press, 1980] 35–38) is much more magnetic, because it concentrates on features of the more striking sayings: (1) they reverse what you expect and they provoke surprise. You don't expect a soft tongue to break a bone (Prov 25:15), or that the bitter turns out to be sweet (27:7). (2) They are provocative; they prompt further thought, and even a contrary proverb. "The one who hesitates is lost" (notice the s and t in this saying; sounds are important), but "look before you leap" (again, notice the combination, lk/lp). These two sayings from our own culture also illustrate the relative measure of truth that is involved in a saying. The proverb is a narrow slice of life, and can be limited by context and audience.

You will find many of the sayings in the book of Proverbs more subtle than you at first think (e.g., see the various translations of 18:21; what attitude to the "tongue" is inculcated?). The difficulty for many readers is that they read them successively, as a piece of prose. But most sayings have to be mulled over. Many are obvious and many are not. Many have to do with moral conduct (the righteous and wicked and their fate), but there are as many that are purely experiential. These simply register a fact; they make an observation about reality without drawing a moral. One has to be ready for surprises. In Proverbs 10–29 there is hardly any context provided, i.e., a context in which one saying is influenced, extended or modified by another. Even the "contradictory proverbs" in 26:4–5; "answer... don't answer...," although they occur in a context in which the "fool" (26:1–12) is constantly mentioned, do not seem to receive any particular slant. Together, they make eminent sense because they complete each other. But even if taken separately, they have independent meaning and do not need each other.

Because the sayings occur in a book of the Bible there is a tendency to look for a moral in them. But a large number are sheer observations; they tell it "the way it is." Such reality therapy was beneficial to youth, introducing them to the facts of life. The context is educational, the message derives from reality. On the other hand, those proverbs which contrast the righteous with the wicked are clearly moralizing. There are others which are value-laden, at least implicitly. Anything that even hints of folly is to be avoided. Success in life depends on carrying out the counsels of the sages.

In the book of Job one will find proverbial sayings embedded in the context of wisdom poems. Thus, Job 6:5 complains in lines that have the ring of a proverb:

> Does the wild ass bray when it has grass?
> Does the bull bellow when it has fodder?

These examples are drawn from the world of nature, and Job uses them to justify his own complaint. Similarly in Ecclesiastes 1:18, after Qoheleth comments on the vanity of wisdom, he supports his statement with a proverb:

> In much wisdom there is much sorrow,
> whoever stores up knowledge stores up grief.

Less frequently there are outright admonitions or commands, backed up by reasons:

> Do not be friendly with the hotheaded,
> nor associate with the angry,
> Lest you learn their ways
> and fall into a trap (Prov 22:24–25).

There are many numerical sayings and also "better"-sayings. Thus:

> Three things are too wonderful for me;
> Four I cannot understand:
> The way of an eagle in the sky,
> The way of a serpent on a rock,
> The way of a ship on the high seas
> and the way of a man with a maiden (Prov 30:18–19).

> Better a dry crust with peace
> than a house full of feasting with strife (17:1).

Many of the proverbs that have come down to us in Western culture are spinoffs from the biblical book. Others have been cultivated by various masters of the aphorism, such as Francis Bacon. And there is hardly a primitive society today that is without its own cache of proverbs: African, Indian, and so forth.

Q. 18. Are there any other collections of proverbs from the ancient world like those in the Bible?

Yes, there are several collections from the ancient Near East: from Sumer, Assyria, Babylonia, and especially from Egypt. This is to be expected. There are not many cultures, modern and ancient, that do not give rise to proverbial sayings. Moreover, as we shall see, in the case of these ancient civilizations, one can also point to the "problem literature," works that resemble the books of Job and Qoheleth. As far as proverbial sayings are concerned, those that have the most pertinence to the Bible are from Egypt. *The Words of Ahiqar*, preserved for us in

Aramaic, derive from an Assyrian background, and show remarkable similarities to biblical sayings.

The most striking discovery linking Israelite and Egyptian wisdom was the publication of the Instruction of the Egyptian sage, Amenemope, in 1923. Remarkable similarities were to be seen between this work and especially Proverbs 22:17–23:11 (cf. *ANET*, 421–24). The dependence of the biblical passage on the Egyptian work seems undeniable, even if the Hebrew poet freely adapted the Egyptian. Unfortunately, a kind of "Egyptianising" of Israelite wisdom began to occur in scholarly writings of this century. The Egyptian Instruction was used (and handed down for the lessons of Egyptian scribes trying to learn the cumbersome script) among the courtiers. This setting came to be transferred to Israel. Were not King Hezekiah and his men mentioned in Proverbs 25:1? Was not the influence of the Egyptian notion of *ma'at* (justice, order, etc.) to be found in the wisdom poems of Proverbs 1–9? It seemed reasonable to associate the Israelite wisdom with a school, the court school in Jerusalem especially, on the analogy of the Egyptian models. But this view has faded considerably. There is no hard evidence for the existence of any schools in Israel, or that wisdom literature grew up only in this ambience. Rather, on the analogy of the proverbial sayings that have been collected from illiterate peoples, there is no reason to go outside of the family and/or tribe for the origins of proverbs. There is no reason to deny that these could have been also cultivated at the court, but the breadth of the sayings in the book of Proverbs is not to be limited to a scribal class. The scholarly dispute between school and family in the educational framework of ancient Israel still goes on (Qoheleth is described in Ecclesiastes 12:9 as a sage who taught the people), and perhaps there is no simple answer.

The many other ancient Egyptian Instructions do reflect a higher class and court atmosphere; they consist mainly in directions for proper conduct (the value of silence and self-control, trustworthiness, and so forth). Oddly, it is only in the late demotic literature that one finds maxims that are combined in the style of the biblical sayings. There are many similarities with the Papyrus Insinger and the Instruction of Anchsheshonq (English translations available in M. Lichtheim, *Ancient Egyptian Literature* [Berkeley: University of California, 1980] III, 159–217).

The Words of Ahiqar (*ANET*, 427–30) have sayings that resemble the style of the sayings in the book of Proverbs. Both works emphasize the disciplining of children (a commonplace in the ancient world), the power, as well as the control, of the tongue, truthfulness, and sayings about the king. In all this there is a general resemblance to Israelite wisdom. There is also a text about personified Wisdom, that is somewhat damaged, but it seems to say that Wisdom is dear to the gods, that she is established in heaven, exalted by the lord of holy ones. The problem with the text is that the term "wisdom" has to be partially restored in the text. With this reading, it is similar to the famous personifications of Wisdom in the book of Proverbs.

Q. 19. What do you mean by the personification of Wisdom?

Notice that I use the word personification. Others prefer the term "hypostasis," or even demi-urge, but I don't think Jewish monotheism can tolerate those terms. There are several personifications in the Bible. In Psalm 85:11 kindness and truth meet; justice and peace kiss. In personification non-human things are treated as if they were human and their actions are described. But there is nothing quite like the personification of Wisdom. She is personified as a woman and in a unique way. I shall skip over the personifications in Proverbs 1 and 9 to concentrate on chapter 8. The chapter opens with Wisdom's call to listen to what she has to say. To this end she describes her prerogatives: sound wisdom, insight, of more value than gold, and so on. But the climax comes in verses 22–31:

> The Lord begot me, the first-born of his ways,
>   the first of his works long ago;
> From of old I was poured forth,
>   at the first, before the earth.
> When there were depths I was brought forth...
>   before the hills I was brought forth;
> When he established the heavens I was there,....
> Then I was beside him as his craftsman,
>   and I was his delight day by day,
> Playing before him all the while,

> playing on the surface of his earth;
> and I found delight in the sons of men. (*NAB*)

Six times Wisdom asserts her primacy at creation, the first of the Lord's acts. What was she doing there? Perhaps assisting in creation, but "craftsman" is an uncertain translation for a word that is also understood to mean "little child." However, it is clear that the occasion is a joyous one (vv 30–31), and she finds her happiness in the human race. That her goal is to be with humankind is indicated in the invitation that follows: "Whoever finds me finds life!" Whether or not she was associated with the Lord in the *act* of creation, she was there as the first-born (born of God! vv 22–23), and her explicit goal is one of joy, with God and especially with humankind. These are unheard-of claims: intimacy with both God and humans—apparently a communication of God to the world. I like the way Ben Sira has picked this up at the opening of his book when he writes that the Lord saw Wisdom and took her measure and

> he poured her out upon all his works,
> upon all the living according to his gift;
> he lavished her upon those who love him (Sir 1:9–10).

In chapter 24 he takes his inspiration from Proverbs 8 and describes how Wisdom originates from the Most High, traverses all creation, and responds to the Lord's command to dwell in Israel—and she does. Now Ben Sira interprets this figure for his generation: she is identified explicitly with the Torah of Moses ("the book of the covenant of the Most High God, the law that Moses commanded us," 24:23).

But the life of Wisdom does not end here. In chapters 7–9 of the Wisdom of Solomon she is described in traits that seem to identify her with Almighty God (7:25–26), yet she is described as sitting by his throne (9:4), with a mission to humankind (7:27). It would appear that she figures again in the New Testament, as a kind of background to the Logos or Word in the gospel of John 1:1–18. Paul calls Jesus "the wisdom of God" in 1 Corinthians 1:14. Hence, there is a growth in the description of this mysterious figure throughout the Bible.

Q. 20. Personified Wisdom is no doubt very important, but isn't it just a small portion of the wisdom literature?

Yes, you are right, but it deserves to be set apart because it is so unusual. Wisdom literature consists of at least five books: Proverbs, Job, Ecclesiastes, Sirach and the Wisdom of Solomon. There is evidence of wisdom influence on other books of the Old Testament, but these five works, by common agreement, are recognized as the wisdom books. Wisdom is personified certainly in four of them; three were mentioned in the last question, and Job 28 would be a fourth. There has even been a suggestion that Wisdom is personified in Ecclesiastes 7:23–29, but this is dubious. These works are classified as wisdom, not just because the word wisdom (*hokmah*) occurs in them, but because of certain other striking characteristics.

The first observation to be made is that none of these works mention the sacred history of Israel. This means that there is a noticeable absence of any reference to the founding of Israel, the patriarchs and the promises, the deliverance at the Exodus, Moses and the Sinai legislation. It is true that the "praise of famous men" in Sirach 44–50 and also the treatment of the plagues in Wisdom 11–19 are exceptions to this statement. But both of them are written at the end of the Old Testament period, and they are exceptions that prove the rule.

The second point is that the sages look at the world from the point of view of experience, and the judgments are all in the light of this perspective. What should one know in order to cope with reality? What is necessary for succeeding in the many settings of life: at work, at home, in conversation, in sorrow and in joy? How is one's conduct to be shaped by these considerations, and what sort of success can be expected? The sages promised success (nothing succeeds like success; and their students needed encouragement—but the sages were not naive about reality).

These concerns sound very worldly, and so they are. But it would be a mistake to consider wisdom as profane or secular in the sense of lacking a religious bent. For example, the first six sentences of the book of Proverbs all deal with this "worldly" aspect of wisdom: discipline, intelligence, conduct, knowledge (which is *never* theoretical, but always practical in this literature) and so forth. These sentences are written to introduce the reader to the corpus of wisdom teachings that follow. Suddenly in verse 7 a central idea appears:

> The fear of the Lord is the beginning of knowledge;
> wisdom and instruction fools despise.

The association of wisdom and fear of the Lord is found several times: Proverbs 9:10; 15:33; Job 28:28; Psalm 111:10. In Proverbs fear of the Lord forms a kind of *inclusio*, appearing again at the end in 31:30. The point of all this is the religious character that pervades Old Testament wisdom. What we consider secular and profane was not so in ancient Israel. It is true that one can single out more obvious "religious" sayings from others. But that does not mean the others have no religious orientation (not even the "table manners" of Sirach 31:12–32:13). In several sayings the sacred name, *yhwh*, appears, while it is absent in others. This is no indication of a distinction between religious and non-religious proverbs. The world of experience was the created world, and the Lord was also the creator.

The third characteristic is the international character of Israelite wisdom. This is in harmony with the first point that was made above, the absence of events from Israel's basic historical foundations. And accordingly, it is exemplified by the similarities that Israelite wisdom shares with the civilizations of the peoples of the ancient Near East, and indeed with many other peoples. No one has a corner on experience and the lessons of experience. But Israel was also able to give her wisdom heritage a particular stamp.

Q. 21. Although you say that the wisdom literature is religious, aren't the proverbs very selfish and self-centered?

Let us consider the first collection (chaps. 1–9) separately from the later collections. It seems as though this collection dates from the post-exilic period and was written expressly as an introduction to the succeeding collections which are almost totally discrete sayings, separate from each other. The religious thrust of these chapters is undeniable. Almost immediately there is a warning against the "sinner" (1:10) who would seduce the youth into murderous and venal pursuits. The preaching of personified Wisdom in this chapter is to warn against such folly. Chapter 2 charts a way (notice how often the word, "way," appears in these chapters): "the way of the good" (v 20) in contrast to the way of the wicked that is the "way of darkness" (2:12; cf. also 4:10–27 for another admonition about the "way"). This is summarized, as it were, in the final chapter where Wisdom issues a call to eat of her food (9:5) in contrast to Dame Folly who promises that stolen water is sweet (9:17). There can be no denying the strong moral thrust present in this introduction which invites the youth to pursue wisdom:

> Then you will understand the fear of the Lord;
>   the knowledge of God you will find;
> for the Lord gives wisdom,
>   from his mouth come knowledge and understanding
>   (2:5–6, *NAB*).

We should recall, too, that this is not speculative knowledge; it is practical conduct that is the goal of wisdom instruction.

However, you rightly point out that there is a self-interest involved in the teaching of the book of Proverbs: if you obey the wise teaching of the sages, you will prosper (cf. 3:3–6); if you refuse it, you will meet with shame and disaster. This is put very clearly, but did it always work? Listen to Proverbs 3:11–12:

> The discipline of the Lord, my son, disdain not;
>   spurn not his reproof;
> For whom the Lord loves he reproves,
>   and he chastises the son he favors (3:11–12, *NAB*).

These lines do more than liken God to a father who must discipline children when the need arises. They display an awareness that prosperity and success are not always the share of the wise person, and one is confronted by the mystery of the love of God which can be a hard discipline and not the easy life that seemed to be promised.

This is a very important point, because the sages are too often written off as naive and unrealistic. They were aware of life's mysteries, the twists and turns that even a good life could be subject to. But they ultimately put their trust in God (3:5, 26), despite the hardships. It is true that more attention is given to the positive advantages of the good way of wisdom, but isn't that to be expected? The essential thing is that they should leave enough room for God to maneuver (they could have been more emphatic about that, I admit). There are two important sayings that indicate they were aware of their own limitations:

> There is no wisdom, no understanding,
>   no counsel, against the Lord.
> The horse is equipped for the day of battle,
>   but victory is the Lord's (21:30–31).

Where the Lord was involved, the wisdom of the sage had to back off, if it were to remain wisdom. More than once the admonition to beware of being wise in your own eyes is expressed (e.g., 3:7), nowhere more pungently than in 26:12:

> You see some who are wise in their own eyes?
>   there is more hope for a fool than for them!

Undergirding this worldview of the sages is an understanding of the Lord as the key agent in everything that happens. No detail escapes the divine attention:

> When the lot is cast into the lap,
>   its decision depends entirely on the Lord (16:33).

We find such a view hard to accept in practice, although we may theoretically grant some ill-defined role to the Lord in all that happens. Moreover, this is not just a quirk of the sage. The view of the Lord's direct involvement with events pervades the entire Old Testament. These ideas form the background to the book of Job, but we will wait until we take up that book before discussing it in more detail.

Now, to your opening claim about the sages. I have tried to defend them against the charge of being simplistic. I cannot deny that they were centered on the self—by the way, that seems to be a rather universal human trait, doesn't it? After all, they aimed at teaching one how to cope with the world and experience. I would also add that self-interest did not blind them from consideration for the neighbor, and especially care for the poor. And as far as personal motivation is concerned, that's a large issue: self-interest tends to assert itself in all we do. Do we act morally solely out of love of God? This question, too, will be explored in the book of Job.

Q. 22. I have noticed a fairly constant repetition of "my son," in the teaching of the sages. Were not women included?

Before trying to answer that question, I would like to make a broad observation about what is called "patriarchalism" (emphasis on the males rather than the females) in the Bible. Frankly, one cannot deny that the Bible is patriarchal in its thrust. This was the nature of the culture of the ancient Near East, and not just of Israel. God's revelation accommodated itself to the situation—the "divine condescension" as St. John Chrysostom called it. This means that the divine revelation has inbuilt limitations, the limitations deriving from those who received it. Their patriarchal culture was simply something that God put up with. We see this in many other features of the ancient biblical world: polygamy, war, etc. God's revelation did not come primarily to lay down rules of conduct but to win peoples to acknowledge God. There is the same kind of "scandal" taken at the particularity of the incarnation. One can ask why did God start with a mission to Abraham? All we can say is that a start had to be made somewhere, and we deal with the historical results. Similarly, because revelation was made in a patriarchal world does *not* mean that men are superior to women, or that the mode of patriarchal society is the model that God intended. God allows human beings to develop, to correct themselves, as in the case of slavery and other evils. It seems to be apparent that in our own time the basic equality of men and women (implicit in Gen 1:27) has asserted itself, and it will remain.

With that as a preliminary, your question prompts the following considerations. (1) Although we know very little about the means of education in ancient Israel, it is safe to say that males were the primary students (a situation that, sadly, marked even recent centuries). (2) The level of general culture, as reflected in the book of Proverbs, can be assumed as standard for women as well. In other words, there is a universal human quality to the teachings that concern both male and female, no matter what the inequalities might have been in the society. The capabilities of the woman described in Proverbs 30:10–31 are utterly remarkable. One may readily grant that the praise of this woman derives from a male point of view, but the poem still says something about the status of women. Perhaps the real issue was power (controlled by males) more than cultural level. Although women who read the Bible today can be put off by the slighting of their position in the Old Testament, the teachings themselves remain pertinent to *both* sexes. Rather, they are deservedly put off by translations of the Bible that refuse to use inclusive gender language—to the extent that the constraints of the English language allow.

In addition, the glorification of personified Wisdom as a women is an important consideration in reply to your question. One must recall that Israel considered *yhwh* as beyond sex, and there was a terrific struggle of loyalty, in which the Canaanite fertility rites played a role. The very first commandments asserted that the Lord was unique and not to be imaged. That imagelessness forbade any likeness (which doubtless would have been in the form of a male deity such as in the pantheon that surrounded Israel). And yet Wisdom is personified as a woman and identified as closely as possible with the Lord, born of God and present before creation, and specifically, any human being. The mystery of Lady Wisdom remains yet to be unravelled (see Q. 19).

Finally, there is a saying from an Egyptian sage, Ptah-hotep, that deserves to be recorded here. He is speaking to males, and his point is that no one is born wise—that good speech is more hidden than precious stones, but it may be found among maids at the grindstones!

Q. 23. What is your favorite proverb?

To be perfectly honest, that is a difficult question to answer. Because the more one studies this book, new lights emerge, and they create, as it were, a new appeal from another favorite. But to answer your question, I think I would say that Proverb 30:18–19 is my favorite. It was quoted above in a reply to Q. 17 as an example of a numerical saying. The poet registers astonishment over four marvelous things, and the fourth is the high point. His wonder deals with "ways"—the way of the eagle in the air, the way of a serpent on a rock, the way of a ship on the high seas, and the way of a man with a maiden. The point is not that in each case no trace is left. Nor can one pin down with surety just which characteristics of an eagle in the air are so appealing. The key to the saying lies in the fourfold repetition of the word, "way." The way in each case is purposeful, but its path is difficult to follow or control. The eagle is on the "way" at any point in traversing through the air; it is not flying without a purpose or goal, without direction. Similarly the serpent on the rock. The point is not how does it move without any legs or anything of that sort. Rather, again, it has its own goal, and pursues it in its (to us) laborious way. Similarly, the ship on the high seas goes on relentlessly to its port. The poet is not interested in explaining the locomotions that one might want to see in all this (fly and not fall, serpent's motion without legs, etc.); these questions would be mere distractions. Rather, there is the mystery of the way to a goal that is pursued, and which is not obvious. The climax comes in the fourth example: the mystery of the attraction between a man and a woman—the path that brings them together, and with such fateful consequences. This "way" embraces a mysterious providence at which the sage marvels. The mysteries of nature serve to enhance the total longing which attracts and binds men and women together. In Genesis 3:16 we read that the desire of the woman is for the man, and in Canticles 7:11 that the man's desire is for the woman.

JOB

Q. 24. Where did the idea of the "patience" of Job come from?

Apparently from the letter of James, 5:11, "You have heard of the *hupomonē* of Job." The Greek word is commonly translated as endurance (*NRSV*) or steadfastness (*NAB*) today and these terms convey the total meaning of Job's experience. It seems that in the seventeenth century the word patience retained more of the overtones of suffering (Latin, *patior*). In fact, the Latin Vulgate read *sufferentiam*, or "suffering" in James 5:11. In any case, in our century, "patience" is too weak a word to describe the character of Job; "endurance" or "steadfastness" is apposite. In the context of James 5, the writer is holding up the example of the suffering of Job and the prophets as models and an encouragement to Christians to persevere.

Q. 25. Did Job really exist?

I think it would be wise to distinguish between the literary Job, the man who is the hero of the book, and the real Job, a person who existed in the dim past of Israel's tradition. In Ezekiel 14 there are two references to Job, and he is bracketed with Noah and Dan(i)el in verses 14 and 20. Noah is, of course, the hero of the Flood (comparable to other heroes in the Mesopotamian stories of the Flood), while the other figure is probably the Danel known from the Canaanite legend. These three came down in the Hebrew tradition as holy men and the Lord is making the point that even if the three were present in Jerusalem now (the beginning of the sixth century) their holiness would save only themselves, no one else. There was a belief in ancient Israel that the presence of righteous people could save a community from destruction (see Gen 18:22–33).

Since Job is bracketed with the other two characters, it might be claimed that there is not much evidence of his existence. But what is more important is that the figure of Job came down in the Israelite tradition as a holy person, a worshipper of the Lord. According to 1:1, "there was a man in the land of Uz, whose name was Job." He is even given a non-Israelite identity, as is also the case with his three friends (Job 2:11). Since wisdom literature is an international phenomenon, this identity should come as no surprise. The real significance of Job is the tradition of holiness which surrounds him. It was such a figure, a righteous man, that was the necessary foil for the author of this book. Hence, I mentioned above the "literary Job." This is the one the reader must engage. The reader should not imagine that the ensuing chapters are a blow-by-blow description of the dispute between Job and the friends. The entire work is a literary composition, behind which stands an author (others might say, authors) of great genius, who chose precisely a holy person as the hero of the book; for his purposes that kind of a choice was necessary.

Q. 26. What is the devil doing in the story?

The devil is not in the story, as you assume. The figure you call the devil is the Satan, or Adversary, or prosecuting attorney, if you will. Notice how this character is introduced: in 1:6 the Lord musters out the heavenly court, the "sons of God" as they are termed in the Hebrew (*NRSV*, "heavenly beings"). These are the members of the heavenly court, who serve the Lord and carry out divine commands (and hence also come to be called angels or messengers). The Lord is not alone in the heavens. There is the court and courtiers with whom God takes counsel (as in Isaiah 6:8, when God asks, "who will go for *us*?"). Among these sons of God is to be found the adversary or Satan who has a specific function to perform. This is brought out by the conversation (1:7; 2:2) that takes place: where have you been?—out patrolling the earth. So here is a servant of the Lord (notice that the Lord is portrayed as asking the Satan where he had come from!), one of the divine family. One may infer that his task is to keep an eye on developments on the earth. At this point the Lord brings up the subject of his faithful servant Job (v 8, which practically repeats v 1, "blameless and upright, fearing God and avoiding evil"). The question of the Satan in verse 9 has been described as the most important question ever voiced in the Bible—and from the mouth of Satan! "Does Job fear God for nothing?" Satan comes right to the point. Perhaps the Lord has been too lenient in this case. Can one be sure of Job's virtue when everything is going his way? The Lord has protected and blessed him at every turn. But try him, and see if he will remain faithful. This is a perennial question among human beings: what is the purity, the selflessness of my love of God? Am I serving God for what I get out of it? It is a question that lasts a lifetime. The Lord accepts the "wager," if it may be called that, and gives Job over to Satan's power. There is a series of announcements of the cataclysmic devastation of all his children and possessions, and Job delivers those memorable words: "The Lord gave and the Lord has taken away, blessed be the name of the Lord." It is important for us to notice that the author explicitly states that Job did not sin (1:22; 2:10). A second scene in the heavenly court follows and the Lord seems even to boast about Job to Satan. The unremitting Adversary wants to turn the screw tighter: touch his person. Then Job suffers from the (unidentifiable) bodily disease that overtakes him for the rest of the book. But he still remains faithful: "Shall we receive the good at the hand of God and not the bad?"

Hence, to answer your question, the Satan is really an agent of the Lord in this prologue of chapters 1–2. You might say that he is suspicious of, perhaps hostile to, human beings—but he seems concerned that God not be deceived by would-be saints. Satan is a figure that grows throughout the Old Testament, and is heard from again in Chronicles (1 Chron 21:1, where he is opposed to God). The malevolent figure of Satan, the devil, appears in the intertestamental and New Testament period.

Q. 27. What is the nature of the agreement between the Satan and the Lord?

I have just called it a "wager," and that is one way of describing the arrangement. Against Satan's claims, the Lord backs Job as a truly loyal servant. Both of them have to wait to see how it will turn out: will Job act as the Satan predicted, or is the Lord's assessment the true one? You might argue that the Lord, who knows all things, knows how it will turn out. But then the arrangement with Satan would not be fair. It is not fair to wager on a sure thing. In order for this to be a test, the Lord has to abide by the rules of the game. The issue of the divine knowledge does not enter into the question.

Q. 28. But if this is a wager, how can anyone believe in a God who treats Job as badly as the Lord does in chapters 1–2?

Whether it is a wager or not, your point is well taken. The Lord comes off looking rather callous, to say the least. When the sincerity of one of his creatures is questioned, the Lord merely delivers him over to heinous suffering—just to see if Job is loyal. Why doesn't the Lord, who must have known how it would end, spare Job such affliction, you might ask? Ah, but then there would have been no book of Job, and no testing of Job. The author has deliberately placed the Lord in a no-win situation. On the one hand, if Satan is given free rein to afflict Job, the Lord seems to be a tyrant, willing to have creatures tortured in order to prove a point. On the other hand, what if the Lord refuses to deal with Satan? Could God really afford to say no to the test? Would it not look as though God were afraid that Satan might be right, and that human creatures are loyal to God because of the divine benefits they receive? That's exactly the ingenious no-win situation which the author of the book of Job has drawn up. Indeed, it is the only way for our love and loyalty for God to be known. Oh, we can claim otherwise, but do we really know the strength of our fidelity and love, the selflessness of our love of God, *without* any testing? This is true in human affairs as well. The thousand little tests between two lovers shows the mettle of their love. Mere talk can conceal typical human selfishness.

Q. 29. Are the friends of Job as foolish as they appear to be?

It is easy to be hard on the three friends. But remember, they are described as being appalled at Job's suffering in 2:13. For a whole week they stay with him without uttering a word, certainly in sympathy. They are provoked by Job's outburst in chapter 3, when he curses the day he was born and asks why he did not die at birth, implicating God in this whole affair (notice that in the dialogues of Job and the friends the sacred name, *yhwh*, is not used; the occurrence in 12:9 seems to be a textual error).

What is the function of the friends in this book? Through them the author articulates the traditional theory of divine justice: God directly gives prosperity to the good, and deals out evil to the wicked. It doesn't matter that some scholars debate this and claim that there is no such retribution, but only a deed/consequence sequence. They would rather say that the order is so set up by God the supervisor, that the good are rewarded and the evil are punished—mechanically and automatically. Both views seem to be found in Old Testament thought. But it all comes down to the same thing. God's justice is defended, and human sinfulness/virtue is given a full accounting. This point of view is found throughout the Old Testament. However, the friends turn it backward, in that they conclude from suffering that sin has been the cause. Hence, in their eyes Job can only be classified as a sinner. He suffers for his wrongdoing. (We may recall that this mentality is also manifested in the New Testament in John 9:2–3). It is true that they see Job's suffering as a trial that leads to repentance and restoration (so Eliphaz in 5:19–21; cf. Prov 3:11–12). In this way the friends attempt to uphold orthodoxy, defending the justice of God. The reader knows better: in view of chapters 1–2, Job is not a sinner. The friends are simply on the wrong track, and they deal out lectures to an innocent man.

It should also be said, however, that the reader must not forget the author who is behind the speeches of the friends. He is marshaling the current theological arguments and gives copious expression to them. Is he guilty of caricature? I don't think so. He himself is not all so secure about what the solution to the mystery of suffering might be. The situation is loaded in favor of Job, because of his integrity—but the friends are kept from knowing that.

Q. 30. Doesn't Job also share his friends' theology of reward/punishment?

Many interpreters of the book claim that this is so. If Job were not suffering, he would be basking in the knowledge that his virtue secures his prosperity. But this is beside the issue. It should be emphasized that Job *never* asks for a return of his goods. In chapter 29 he gives a vivid description of the prosperity he once enjoyed. This does not have the ring of, "I deserved it; give it back." Rather, Job is simply devastated by the lack of any relationship with the God whom he served. In chapter 23 he laments that he cannot find God: Whatever point of the compass he turns to, he cannot find God, that very God who knows Job's way (23:8–10). Hence, his total discouragement, even despair. Yes, Job judges his personal relationship to God in virtue of what happens to him. But what other criteria can he use? It is certainly not the crass "do this, and get that" (and vice versa) which the friends advocate in the name of orthodoxy. His relationship with the Lord has been destroyed. This personal attitude can be seen in such passages as 7:7–8, "Remember that my life is but a breath; my eyes will never again see happiness. The eye that beholds me will see me no more; your eye will seek me, but I will be gone!" It is quite remarkable that while the friends never address God directly, Job nearly always concludes his responses to them with a fairly lengthy address to God. This is conspicuous in the first part of the debate.

Q. 31. Is it not a fact that Job despairs of God?

Yes, that is true. You can single out various statements of this desperate man: "If I appealed to him and he answered me, I could not believe that he would listen to my words" (9:16). And there are the apparently blasphemous statements in 9:22–24, "Both the innocent and the wicked he destroys...he laughs at the despair of the innocent...." But despair is not to be captured in one statement or another. It is a mood which finds expression, even while it is undergirded by faith. Job goes from one extreme to another, ceaselessly. I don't think it is fair to catch him at one point and argue that he has despaired. The human psyche is too complicated for snapshot views. Job fluctuates between despair and faith—which is exactly the impression that the brilliant author wished to create, because it is a realistic trait of human life. More than once Job expresses the desire to have a confrontation with God (and in the end, he will); these go counter to any permanent despair.

Q. 32. What do you mean by the "integrity" of Job?

This can mean several things. First of all it describes Job's relationship to the Lord in 1:1, which the Lord takes up again in 1:8. Second, the integrity of Job, as the author has planned this in the book, is Job's refusal to go along with the frozen and faulty theology of the friends. The siren song of orthodoxy is rejected in favor of honesty. Job is assured that if only he would admit his sinfulness and have recourse to the mercy of the Lord, he would be healed, and what's more, enjoy the prosperity that belongs to the righteous (see 5:19–27; 8:6–7; 11:13–19 and Elihu in 33:19–30). Here is the dilemma the author has created for Job: Job would be dishonest were he to mouth the platitudes uttered by the friends. He has also let the reader know that Job is innocent. So the theology of the friends is off the mark, and the heavy burden of struggling with this mysterious God is upon Job's shoulders.

You might reply to this that Job seems to admit to some sinfulness, as in 7:21 when he asks God, "Why do you not pardon my offense and take away my iniquity?" (cf. also 13:26). I think that these are rhetorical flourishes which Job does not take seriously, because in chapter 31 (and cf. 27:2–6) he takes several oaths affirming sinlessness. Thus he can attack God, whom he accuses of searching out his sins, "even though you know that I am not guilty" (10:7). The sinfulness and weakness of every human being are basic data in Old Testament thought. That, too, weighs on Job's mind (or should one more accurately say that it is given expression by the author through Job?), but his constant affirmation of innocence prevails over all. One might also ask if the author felt that he had to be perfectly logical in the last analysis. Would not an innocent man so wildly tormented as Job wonder what the meaning of integrity is? And would not the outcries of Job gain reality by the fact that in the portrait of the sufferer there is an echo, however faint, of the sinfulness that afflicts humankind and is so vividly portrayed in the laments of the psalmists? Job is, as it were, an archetypal sufferer.

Q. 33. Doesn't Job say "my redeemer liveth," showing he believes in the afterlife?

With those famous words you are alluding to Job 19:25–27, perhaps the most difficult and mysterious passage in the whole Bible. I say that not to avoid a difficulty, but to point out a fact which you can verify yourself by consulting various translations. Indeed, the introductory phrase, "my redeemer liveth" may be known to most people because of its appearance in Handel's *Messiah*, rather than because of its place in the Bible. Moreover, the word redeemer casts a Christian aura about the passage. At least, Christians are tempted to think of Christ and the resurrection. Of course, these verses do not and cannot refer to Christian beliefs. There are several reasons why this is so, even if the text has been injured in its transmission. First, the word translated as "redeemer" is *gōʾēl*, which means one who is next-of-kin, and has the duty to come to the aid of a relative. Now that is a saving action and may well involve a transaction that involves a redemption (from debt, from captivity, etc.). "Vindicator" is a better translation in the context. Job affirms that he has a vindicator, a champion, who will prove Job right and just in the end (despite the accusations of the friends). Who is this vindicator? I think it is the God with whom he has been arguing and pleading throughout the debate. Others think some unspecified intercessor is meant. The question is not easy to solve. But here Job calls special attention to the importance of his proclamation. He wants these words to be written down, not cast headlong into the air, incised in a rock forever with an iron pen and lead so that it could never disappear (19:23–24). In 16:19 he speaks of a "witness" in heaven, perhaps an intercessor (cf. 5:1), perhaps God. As it were he appeals to God against God. But in 19:25 the identity of the vindicator is much clearer. Second, although the text is unsteady, Job seems to refer clearly to some event in the end when he will *see* the vindicator. There is a remarkable emphasis on Job's eyes and vision (vv 26–27). It is not clear just when this vision will take place ("at the last"—the last of what?). The entire passage is a monumental affirmation of faith in the integrity of God, his judge, as well as in his own integrity.

The idea of the resurrection of the body does not seem to appear in the Bible until the time that Daniel was written (in the second century; cf. Dan 12:2–3 and the books of Maccabees). The vision in Ezekiel 37 pictures a resuscitation of the dry bones in the valley where the spirit of the Lord sets the prophet down. But the bones are explained: "These bones are the whole house of Israel" (37:22). The vision deals with the revival of the people of God, not with personal resurrection. Moreover, if Job had a belief in an afterlife, this might have alleviated somewhat his situation. At least, it would have changed the game plan of the author. But the fact is that there is no meaningful afterlife for Job. There is only Sheol (see Q. 8 above) to which he alludes many times, but usually with a sad note, as the place where he must eventually go (e.g., 10:21–22). Although Sheol paradoxically also serves as a place of respite, a corner where the Lord might overlook him (cf. 3:11–19; 10:18–20; 14:13).

Finally, one might see this famous passage of chapter 19 as the climax of previous statements in which Job has spoken of, even yearned for, a confrontation with God (however hopeless it might seem to be; cf. 9:20; 13:3; 16:22). This may be the author's ironic anticipation of the vision of God that Job will experience later (38:1–42:5).

Q. 34. How does the poem on searching for Wisdom in chapter 28 fit into the book?

This famous chapter really deals with the "not finding" of Wisdom: "where can Wisdom be found?" (v 12, with a refrain in v 20). In short, the author of this poem tells us that although human beings can penetrate the depths of the earth and find precious stones, they cannot find Wisdom. In their search they are answered on all sides: the Abyss and the Sea claim that they don't have it; Abaddon and Death say that they have merely heard of Wisdom. Finally, an answer is given: God knows where it is. Since God sees everything that is under the heavens (vv 23–24), that is a logical answer. Moreover, in 28:27 the author describes how God saw it, and searched it out. The difficulty is that nowhere is it stated where God put it. The divinity knows the way to it, but no human being can find where it is!

Such a poem has puzzled the interpreters of Job, and deservedly so. Of itself, this chapter fits with other portions of the Old Testament where Wisdom is personified (see Q. 19), although the figure in chapter 28 is not described as female. Moreover, one can ask whether this chapter is really attributed to Job by the author. Job speaks chapters 26 and 27 (see the introduction in 26:1), but the last 11 verses in chapter 27 are very difficult to fit into Job's viewpoint. Then, unannounced, appears the poem on Wisdom, which does not betray the agony of Job's previous speeches. Chapter 28 comes like a bolt out of the blue. Then Job is introduced as speaking in 29:1. Some interpreters consider chapter 28 an "interlude," but such terminology is a coverup of the problem of sequence.

Here is an attempt at a solution. Suppose you write several chapters about a mysterious phenomenon in human history—such as retribution was for Israel, and still remains for the modern believer. Suppose further that your efforts to make sense of God's doings fall short of conviction. Honesty would compel you to admit your failure—that the requisite wisdom is beyond human reach. That seems to be the *function* of this poem on Wisdom. Whether the author of the book or another was the poet makes little difference. The effect of the poem is to say that the answer to the question that is being debated is ultimately not to be had. God alone knows the answer. This does not mean that the rest of the book can be dismissed. Rather, it is a claim for mystery, and the need to acknowledge the mystery.

Thus far I have limited myself very deliberately to the Wisdom poem, 28:1–27, and have avoided mentioning the final verse of the chapter, which runs: "And he (presumably God) said to humankind: Behold the fear of the Lord (*Adonai*) is wisdom and avoiding evil is understanding." What does this mean? First of all, it doesn't seem to be part of the poem that goes to great length to associate Wisdom with God. Second, it could be an addition that ties the poem in with 1:1 by repeating the phraseology used to describe Job's virtue. "Fear of the

Lord" is, of course, a central concept of the wisdom literature (see Q. 64), and it is given a strong moral connotation by being coupled with the avoidance of evil. Third, the meaning of the statement in this context seems to be that the moral deportment of human beings is the answer to the problem of Job (even if Job is not convinced!). The issue is not an intellectual one, but a moral one which humans solve by a proper attitude toward God. That is the only answer! Hence, if I have explained the chapter correctly, the final verse says that the mystery remains, but one's relationship with God counts above all the theologizing.

Q. 35. How do you understand God's "answer" to Job (chaps. 38–42)?

Notice that this question skips over the discourse of Elihu in chapters 32–37. I can understand why. In chapters 29–31 Job stops talking to the friends. He once more describes his misery and then turns on God in a final word that lays down the gauntlet: "let the Almighty answer me!" (31:35). Just at this point one might expect a divine intervention, if ever the Lord is going to make an appearance. Instead we meet Elihu who carries on the debate in four speeches because he is dissatisfied with the way in which the friends have argued with Job. He proposes to set that right, but it is difficult to see that he adds anything to their arguments. He elaborates the role of human suffering in the plan of divine providence: it is medicinal (33:19–33; 36:8–15). But he really says nothing new. It is hard to explain why Elihu appears here. In a sense he prepares for the appearance of the Lord, but there doesn't seem to be any need for preparation. Indeed, the beautiful creation hymn of 36:26–37:24 steals a bit of God's thunder! Job doesn't even bother to answer him.

Finally comes the answer out of the whirlwind (a re-creation of the Old Testament understanding of the theophany), as the Lord speaks (the sacred name, *yhwh*, is used for the first time since the prologue in chapters 1–2): "Where were you when I laid the foundations of the earth?...." Thus begins a series of unanswerable questions that are put to Job in such a manner as to overwhelm him. Perhaps we can distinguish between the substance and the style of the questioning. The substance indicates the ability of the author to present an interesting portrayal of creation quite different from Genesis 1. The style is more gentle than it first appears. Only once is the Lord clearly sarcastic, as in 38:21—you know how I did these things for you were born then! (we know from Proverbs 8:22–31 that only Wisdom was present when the Lord created, and Job was far down the line!).

But readers find the questions about creation quite disconcerting. Job has several times cried out, "Why?" Yet he receives no rational answer from the Lord. Obviously the author felt that no "answer" was available. The fact of the matter is that no "answer" to the suffering of the righteous is yet available after all these years. Suffering remains a mystery. What, then, has the author chosen to do? With remarkable poetic verve he has described the "marvels" of God's creating the heavens and the earth. But it is quite the opposite of those creation hymns, where humans play a large role (Pss 8; 139:13–16). Here creation itself is the marvel, and the care that God expends upon humans is played down. There is a certain prodigality in the provision of rain in uninhabited areas (38:26), and in the speed of the dumb ostrich (39:17–18). The reaction of Job can only be described as cautious (40:3–5): he must be silent. It is only very briefly and almost incidentally that the substantial question appears: "Will you condemn me that you may be justified?" God asks of Job (40:8). Only if Job has an arm like God, or can thunder with the voice of God—in other words, if he can truly rule over the universe! The impossibility of Job's doing this is shown in these speeches. The chaos monsters, Behemoth and Leviathan, are mere creatures of God, made just as God made Job (40:13) and totally servants of the Lord (41:4). God has not destroyed them, as they might deserve. They are the most expressive symbols of evil, and remain as mysterious in the divine designs as evil itself.

Thus far, we may characterize God's "answer" as a refusal to answer. No rational explanation is given. The Lord has intervened and appeared to Job, and Job has survived it! The same Job who has been very hard-headed in his arguments with the Three, giving no quarter, and clearly challenging God, now surrenders:

> I had heard of you by word of mouth—
> but now my eye has seen you (42:5)

This reaction of Job is not to be separated from the speeches of the

Lord; indeed it is integral to them. The author of the work presents an encounter with God, a vision or experience that is expressed verbally in the speeches and comes to a climax in Job's surrender. It is often said that the only "answer" that the book provides lies in these verses. I think the book has much more than this to say, but 42:5 is surely important: it shows Job's transformation.

I wish that the meaning of 42:6 was as clear as 42:5. Most translations have it that Job somehow draws back from the position he has taken in the book and repents in dust and ashes. But this is highly unlikely. The translation of 42:6b is the problem. It is frequently rendered as "repent in dust and ashes" (*NRSV* and many others). But the normal meaning of *nhm'l*, found elsewhere in the Bible is to "repent concerning" and usually indicates a change of mind. Hence, one cannot "repent in." In 42:6b one can understand Job despising himself (so *NRSV*). But how can he go on to say that he repents in dust and ashes, in view of the Lord's statement in the next verse? In 42:7 the Lord says that Job has spoken rightly in contrast to the three friends who have not. They provoke the divine wrath and Job is told to intercede for them. As we have seen (Q. 32), the very integrity of Job calls for honesty and truthfulness in his reactions. He cannot go back on that! What has he to be sorry for? Some interpreters have thought that Job is repenting of the excessive language, the bitter attacks that he launched against the Almighty. But this is not said in the text; it is an assumption made to avoid the difficulty. We can conclude that "repentance in dust and ashes," which can only mean sorrow for some wrongdoing (e.g., Job's language) is ruled out by divine verdict. I would offer the following translation:

> Therefore I despise myself and relent,
> being but dust and ashes.

"Dust and ashes" does not necessarily connote penance. It can designate simply the human condition, a sign of human frailty, as Abraham before God in Genesis 18:27. And in Job 30:19, the same phrase seems to indicate Job's creatureliness (cf. Job 10:9). Here in 42:6 Job is simply acknowledging his status as a human being before God. He has done this before, in a different mood, as when he reminded God that the creator's care for him should reflect something of the concern that went into the act of creation (10:8–17).

Q. 36. What do you call the literary form of the book of Job?

Its literary form has been described as *sui generis* (M. Pope)—as unique. There is really nothing that can quite compare with it. It embraces all manner of individual and lesser forms and subordinates these to a greater whole. For example, one might agree easily that the literary form of chapter 3 can be matched by the laments in the psalter or in Jeremiah (e.g., Jer 12:1–4). It has the despairing mood of Psalm 88 or Jeremiah 15:10, "Woe is me, mother, that you ever bore me...." Because of the many complaints, and the dialogue that ensues, the work has been described as the "dramatization of a lament" (C. Westermann). This is helpful in understanding a major thrust of the book. Others have claimed that the book is the reflection of a judicial process. It has also been termed a "paradigm of an answered complaint," on the analogy of a Mesopotamian work named, "I will praise the Lord of Wisdom" (see Q. 39). All of these attempts have some value in that they seize on one or another aspect of the work. This itself is a sign that no one characterization is satisfactory. The book combines several literary forms drawn from wisdom and legal dispute.

Q. 37. I have heard the book of Job described as comedy and as irony. Would you comment on this?

In this context comedy does not mean a funny story. It is rather a classical term to designate the mixture of the ironic and the incongruous, all the while a basic story line is followed that in the end provides happiness for the hero. Incongruity appears in the Lord's admission to the Satan that "you have incited me against him without cause" (2:3). Job will develop this "injustice" of God in his speeches—why has the supposedly just God treated him badly? But there is also the incongruity in Job himself: the difference between the resigned Job of the prologue and the rebel of the dialogue. The incongruities and ironies can be seen in the following considerations (which are far from being exhaustive).

1. The rebellious Job is restored, but the spokesmen for God are rejected.
2. Love of God is shown by an innocent person who suffers the fate of the wicked.

3. The friends say many things to Job that, ironically, will be verified, but not in the way they expected:

- Bildad in 8:6–7 says that God will care for Job if he is blameless.
- Job in 9:17 says that God wounds him "without cause" (as God admitted to the Satan in 2:3).
- Zophar says to Job in 11:5: Would that God might speak to you and reveal the secrets of wisdom. That will happen!
- Eliphaz in 22:3 derisively asks Job whether Shaddai, the Almighty, will gain if he is righteous. According to the prologue, Shaddai will gain, defeating Satan's claim.
- Eliphaz in 22:27–30 tells Job that God will listen to Job's prayers; indeed this happens; cf. 42:9, where God accepts Job's intercession for the friends.

4. There is a double edge to the speeches of the Lord; they can be interpreted as sarcastic, even as ridiculing Job. And yet... The Lord has to take Job on with such long (and irrelevant?) speeches, almost as if Job were at least a member of the heavenly court (cf. 1:6). In the mind of many readers, the testing of Job has become a testing of God.

5. There is a paradoxical edge to the vision of God (42:5). Job has complained that he cannot see God (9:11; 23:8–9), and when the breakthrough comes it is in a vision!

6. Perhaps the ultimate irony is the "happy ending" since it leaves so many things in the book unexplained.

It makes little difference what terminology is used to describe the genre of the book. The important thing is that the readers leave themselves open to the ambiguities and ironies which characterize Job's journey, a journey into transformation.

Q. 38. What would you say is the meaning of the book of Job?

There is no one meaning; there are several meanings. I would begin with the presupposition that the book as a whole does not pretend to give a definitive answer to anything, or to limit itself to one point of view. I would describe the various meanings: 1. A challenge to religion: is a disinterested piety viable, or does one serve God in order to receive divine blessings? 2. The reasoning of the friends is wrong; one cannot argue that adversity and suffering are a sign of wrongdoing. 3. To give chapter 28 its due, it seems to say there is no "reason" or explanation that can be advanced for Job's plight (or the suffering of any innocent person). 4. Job's affirmation of a vision of God (42:5) speaks to the experience of those who endure suffering in faith—because they, too, have a vision, an experience of God that enables them to persevere. 5. The "happy ending," far from being the main point of the book, or as some would argue a major correction of the book's trend, has a function. God *does* bless those who are loyal. But there is not always a happy ending. Within the structure of the book it witnesses to a fact, but not to the frequency or to the manner of the fact. Throughout all these questions I have been treating the book as a whole, and not speculating about the genesis of the work, i.e., how many authors may be responsible for it. Even if there are good arguments to consider the prologue and the epilogue as separate from the dialogue and written by another hand, it is the book in its present form (however dislocated it might seem to be in parts) that calls for explanation.

Q. 39. Are there any characters in the rest of the Bible or in the ancient world that resemble Job?

In the broad sense of resemblance, I would suggest that the experience of Abraham in Genesis 22 is similar. In both cases there is a test, and the situation of the one being tested is unbearable. Abraham's test goes far beyond the suffering caused by his paternal instincts in the fulfillment of the command to slay Isaac. Child sacrifice was not uncommon in the patriarchal culture of old. The real test is whether or not Abraham can take seriously this God in view of past events. He has been promised a family (indeed, a nation), a land, and also somehow his name will be blessing to all (Gen 12:1–3). But as we read through Genesis we learn that Abraham is too old, and also Sarah is sterile. Abraham tries to persuade God to fulfill the promise made to him by making Eliezer his heir—but he is refused. Similarly, when Ishmael is born of Hagar, there is the same plea; let Ishmael be the child of promise. But no—it has to be God's way. The promise is reiterated several times. Finally, it is fulfilled in the birth of Isaac—and now he is to be sacrificed! What kind of a God is this? Abraham does not agonize, as Job does. But the reader can agonize, and the effect is similar.

Many of the unknown psalmists have voiced complaints and recriminations against God that remind one of Job. Hence the suggestion was made in Q. 36, that the book of Job was "the dramatization of a lament." There was, therefore, a rich tradition of lament and complaint that the book of Job is the heir to.

Another character that can be suggested is the unnamed and unknown servant in Isaiah 52:13–53:12. The servant doesn't speak, but we learn from those who observe and describe him that he suffered innocently, that he was despised and cut off from all. The new and surprising element, not found in the book of Job, is that the suffering of this servant is redemptive, that it is for the sake of others. This is stated several times: "He was wounded for our transgressions, crushed for our iniquities; upon him was the punishment that made us whole, and by his bruises we were healed" (Is 53:5). This trait, that suffering can be a healing for others, is unique to this poem, and increases all the more the mystery that confronted Job.

In the ancient world, two literary pieces have been compared in a special way with Job. The first is the Akkadian *Ludlul bel nemeqi* (I Will Praise the Lord of Wisdom, *ANET*, 434–37). The main similarity is that the hero claims to be righteous and yet is suffering. There is no dialogue or debating about the ways of God and humans. It is rather a thanksgiving that praises Marduk because he delivers the one who was suffering. In other words, the complaint is answered, and the individual is restored. But the agony of Job is simply not to be found here. Moreover, it stands to reason that there must have been plenty of people who felt that suffering was undeserved, and therefore could only blame God. But Job cannot be reduced simply to that level; there is no question of dependence.

The second is *The Babylonian Theodicy*, also called *The Dialogue about Human Misery*. This is a dialogue between the one who is suffering and his friend, but it has none of the passion and sharpness of the Joban dialogue. The friend is gentle in trying to bring the sufferer back into a better relationship with God and also sounds a note that is found in the three friends: Wrongdoing will not achieve anything; one must be faithful to one's god. However, it is admitted that the gods made the human race sinful. An admission like this destroys any kind of similarity with the story of Job.

One may conclude that suffering is surely a frequent topic in all the ancient writings. Reality would seem to guarantee that. But similarities between these writings and Job are not great, and ultimately they are meaningless. We all think we suffer unjustly at some time or other.

Q. 40. Has the book of Job really influenced great thinkers such as philosophers and theologians, poets and artists?

Indeed it has. The recent commentary of D. Clines (*Job 1–20*, WBC 17; [Dallas: Word, 1989]) has an "orientation" to books about Job that takes up over 50 pages. It is not simply a record of the classic commentaries such as the *Moralia* of Gregory the Great, but the broader picture of the influence which the book has had in art, music, dance, film, etc. There are several modern plays which have been inspired by the book. My favorite, although it is not quite a play, is the long dramatic poem by the late New England poet, Robert Frost, entitled "The Masque of Reason." At the outset of the poem Job and his wife are speaking together; Job has recovered from his suffering although he still feels some effects from it all. Suddenly a figure approaches, Job's wife recognizes that it is the Lord, crying out that she would know him anywhere from Blake's pictures! (William Blake, the English poet, illustrated the book of Job with several famous drawings.) When Job tries to engage the Lord in conversation, the Lord interrupts, and expresses a desire to thank Job, who has been a divine concern over the years. Thanks are due to Job for his help in freeing God from bondage to a theoretical principle—that there must be a connection between what people do and the reward or punishment they receive. Using the jargon of biblical scholars, the Lord tells Job that the Deuteronomist has been proved wrong (a reference to the theology of Deuteronomy which emphasizes reward/punishment according to human conduct). God had been placed in a box, as it were, having to react automatically in line with orthodox theory. Instead, Job set God free, free to reign, to be God. I recommend this work of Robert Frost to you; it is a good commentary on the biblical work.

SONG OF SONGS

Q. 41. What is the correct title for the Song of Songs?

The Hebrew title given to it in the Jewish tradition strikes me as the correct one: *shir hashirim*, or Song of Songs. This is Hebrew idiom for the superlative, like "king of kings," or the greatest king. So also, this is the greatest song. This was rendered in the Latin tradition as *Canticum canticorum*, and hence "Canticle of Canticles." Because of the association of Solomon with the poem it has come to be called "The Song of Solomon." However, this is misleading. Although Solomon is mentioned several times in the eight chapters of the book, he is never represented as speaking. I wouldn't lay too much stress on the word, "song." It could very well be that passages in the book were put to music, but we have no firsthand evidence of that. There certainly are poems of various kinds and these have been assembled together in a loose unity of dialogue.

Q. 42. How many characters are there in the book?

You can certainly count a woman and a man and Daughters of Jerusalem. An unidentified party seems to speak the last two lines in 5:1. Some would argue that there are two men, not one. There is a man who is called a king (cf. 1:4, 12), and identified with Solomon by many, and another man who seems to be a shepherd (cf. 1:7–8). These characters are then described by some interpreters as suitors for the hand of the maiden. There would be some suspense, supposedly, in the maiden's choice. Will she yield to the blandishments of the king, or will she be faithful to her rustic lover? I think this is a misinterpretation of the Song. Such a scenario is built up by the imagination of interpreters who supply their own stage directions for this dramatic unfolding of events. The Song is dramatic, but not a drama; it is a series of love poems that have been arranged to form a dialogue, mainly between a man and a woman. There is only one man, who is identified now as a king and now as a shepherd, in these poems. This is not unusual in the imagination of lovers. It is an accepted literary fiction to identify the beloved with various characters, just as the woman is called "sister," and "bride" (4:9–12).

Q. 43. I have a hard time following the dialogue; how can you tell who is speaking and to whom?

In some translations, such as the *NAB* and the *NEB*, the identity of the speakers are given by marginal indications: the woman, the man, and the Daughters of Jerusalem. This sort of practice was utilized in ancient Greek manuscripts. How certain is it? I would say well over ninety percent. One will find differences among translators, but by and large the identities are secured by the gender indications of the Hebrew text. It is these grammatical signs that distinguish between masculine and feminine and singular and plural that make possible a virtual certainty concerning the speakers in most instances.

If there are no marginal indications, then a reader of the English Bible will find more confusion than expected. In some individual cases one can tell that a man speaks, and in others that a woman speaks. For example, when the woman says that she seeks him whom her soul loves (3:1–4), there can be no doubt.

Sometimes it is clear that a conversation is going on, as in 5:8–9 when the woman asks the Daughters to tell her lover that she is faint with love. They reply immediately with words (v 9) that are practically an invitation for her to describe her lover—what is so extraordinary about him?

There is also the problem, to *whom* one is speaking. Often the woman seems to be giving a soliloquy. Thus, in 2:4–7 she describes how her lover brought her to the banquet, and she launches into an appeal to the Daughters (2:4–7). Are they really present in a physical sense, or are they merely a fictional part of the soliloquy? This is often difficult to determine, and it may depend on the way in which one has already construed the action and dialogue in the Song. The *New Oxford Annotated Bible* has made an effort in the footnotes to make these identifications.

Q. 44. What is the meaning of the Song of Songs?

One might ask, what is the meaning of love poetry? When a man writes a poem or sings a song to a woman—or vice versa—the meaning lies in the affective expressions of desire, joy, descriptions, teasing, the motifs of presence/absence of the beloved, and the many other shades of the language of love. One can call this a celebration of human sexual love. This kind of literature is illustrated in both ancient and modern times. The love poetry which has the greatest affinity with the Song of Songs is that of Egypt. Several collections of Egyptian love poems have been published, and the similarity to the biblical Song is rather obvious. There is a "common atmosphere of sensual pleasures: seeing, hearing, touching, smelling, tasting. And the environment of love they depict similarly abounds with perfumes, spices, fruits and flowers, trees and gardens" (R. E. Murphy, *The Song of Songs: A Commentary* [Hermeneia; Minneapolis: Fortress, 1990] 46). In the Egyptian poems the lovers refer to each other as "brother" and "sister"—in the Song the woman is called "my sister, my bride." The most striking difference between Egypt and Israel in this regard is that the Egyptian poems are separate units, not united by dialogue. The man and the woman do not talk to each other but about each other. This is in sharp contrast to the dialogical character of the Song.

Such comparisons as these aid us in understanding the meaning of the Song. It deals with human sexual love. Indeed, one has merely to read the opening line of the Song, "Let him kiss me with the kisses of his mouth," to be aware of this.

What was behind the collection of these songs (no matter what their dates may have been)? The work is more than a haphazard anthology. There are enough signs to indicate that the editor (who may also have been the author, or chief author) found a certain unity in the work and in its message. Who would have been responsible for the transmission and preservation of the Song? One can only speculate, but several modern scholars have looked to the wisdom tradition as the area most congenial to the ideals of the Canticle. Elsewhere in the Bible love between the sexes is viewed primarily in terms of procreation. The Song fills a lacuna in the wisdom teaching by emphasizing the joy that man and woman can find in each other. For example, most of the discussion of women in Proverbs is couched in terms of a warning about the "strange" woman. Proverbs 5:15–20 is the exception and its terminology is reminiscent of the Song. One of the sayings in Israel recognized the importance of a loving spouse:

> Whoever finds a wife finds happiness;
> and receives favor from the Lord (Prov 18:22).

Q. 45. Isn't it shocking to find such sexy songs in the Bible?

The answer to that is a simple NO. Think of the implications of that question. It would imply that sex is something to be ashamed of. But sex is precisely the creation of God, and therefore worthy to be found in the literature inspired by God. Moreover, the language in the Song is restrained rather than prurient. It creates an atmosphere, such as the references to gardening, to graceful animals, etc., that deliberately have a double meaning, that suggest more than they actually describe. Yes, the language is erotic, because eros or love is the subject of the poetry. In fact, the Song exhibits a sound and healthy attitude to sex, and it can form the basis of an appreciative attitude needed in a society that degrades sex. There is a reverence in its sexuality, and this is further strengthened by the mutuality of the love between the man and the woman and their fidelity to each other.

Q. 46. I have heard that the Song of Songs should be interpreted allegorically; what do you think of the allegorical meaning?

Some words about allegory need be said: no literature *must* be interpreted allegorically. If a work is written as an allegory, then an allegorical interpretation is in order. One must determine from the work whether or not its intent is allegorical; only such arguments can demonstrate the nature of the work. Now, can this be applied to the Song of Songs?

Allegorical interpretation has been very popular in the history of the exegesis of the Bible. Around the time of Christ, Philo of Alexandria was famous for his allegorical interpretation, and in the Jewish tradition the Song of Songs was interpreted allegorically. The Targum, or Aramaic paraphrase, of the Song understands it as an historical allegory, describing important events from the Exodus through to the diaspora in the Christian era. The allegorical approach (God and the people of Israel) has been dominant in the Jewish tradition. In the Christian understanding of the Song, Origen set the tone. The eight chapters deal with God and people, i.e., Christ and the church. Origen does not deny a literal historical meaning; he even presents it, but he goes beyond it, for he thinks the true meaning deals with Christ and the church, and especially Christ and the individual soul. This mystical bent was developed considerably in the later tradition of the church, especially in the writings of

St. Bernard of Clairvaux, who has left 86 sermons (to the monks at Clairvaux) on the Canticle, and he covered only the first two chapters! In contrast to Origen, who did pay attention to a basic literal sense, Bernard explored only the ascetical and mystical meanings of the Song, correlating the text with the spiritual dimensions of human experience. Indeed the twelfth century was the century of the Song of Songs, with more works being written about it than about any other Old Testament book. This interpretation continued through the Reformation and on into modern times. Among the remarkable works of Spanish literature are the short poems of St. John of the Cross, such as the *Spiritual Canticle*, that are filled with unmistakable allusions to the Song, even without explicitly identifying the love theme as the love of God.

It is helpful to distinguish between the spiritual meaning and the allegorical interpretation. I would argue that the spiritual meaning is a valid dimension of the biblical work. But the allegorical interpretation is at fault because it employs allegorical methodology when this is not appropriate. Let me give an example. The commentary of the great French exegete, André Robert, interprets Canticle 7:4 concerning the breasts of the woman as referring to Mt. Ebal and Mt. Garizim. Allegory, too, often has sinned by excess (see also Q. 49 for further discussion of the spiritual meaning of the Song).

Q. 47. You mention two meanings of the Song of Songs—a literal sense of love between the sexes and a spiritual meaning that deals with the love between God and human beings. Can you have it both ways?

Yes, that is correct. I think that the literal historical meaning is clear enough from the obvious sense of the words in the Song. Moreover, it is a message that needs to be heard in our day. It is a portion of the Bible whose voice has too long been drowned out by the heavy weight of tradition.

I don't think that the spiritual meaning has to be defended. First, all literature, of whatsoever kind, is subject to extended meaning. Thus we interpret the constitution of the United States, or the works of Shakespeare, and arrive at meanings that the original authors did not have in mind. This is nothing new.

Second, there is the astounding historical fact that both the synagogue and the church interpreted the Song in a sense other than the literal sense which I have called "obvious." This agreement in interpretation between the two communities of faith which transmitted and preserved the Song is not to be dismissed lightly. This example from Origen can illustrate the search for a fuller understanding of the mysterious Song. In explaining 2:9–14 he comments on 2:12–13 ("The winter is past...the blossoms appear in the land...") that it is the season of spring, and a fitting time for the bride to come forth. This is an adequate comment from a literal-historical point of view. But then Origen goes on to say that this reading of the text is not adequate because it offers no profit to the reader, and that it is necessary to find the spiritual meaning here. In other words, Origen was trying to apply an ancient text to the current situation as he understood it. This is a move that all interpreters make. No one remains anchored in an immovable point in the historical past. That point is the beginning of interpretation, not the end. See also Q. 48.

Third, there is precedent for the spiritual meaning within the Old Testament itself. "You shall be my people and I shall be your God." This central affirmation of the covenant relationship was spelled out in several ways. One way was that of law. The people of God were expected to be faithful to the covenant demands (the Decalogue, etc.). But law is not the only metaphor employed. The prophets especially used the metaphor of marriage. There is a marriage, a relationship of intimate love, between *yhwh* and the people. Fidelity to God is then portrayed in terms of the marriage bond. A striking presentation is found in Hosea 1–3. Although there is a bitter indictment of Israel for infidelity, one also finds those soothing words: "I will espouse you to me forever; I will espouse you with righteousness and justice, in love and in mercy...in faithfulness" (Hos 2:18–19). Even though the metaphor is often used to score the infidelity of the people, it faces toward the future, as in Isaiah 62:5:

> As a young man marries a virgin,
> your Builder shall marry you;
> And as a bridegroom rejoices in his bride
> so shall your God rejoice in you (*NAB*).

With this kind of tradition concerning the Lord and Israel as background, one can understand more readily how the traditional spiritual meaning became so fixed in both Christian and Jewish tradition. The statement attributed to Rabbi 'Aqiba rings true: "all the ages are not worth the day on which the Song of Songs was given to Israel; for all the Writings are holy, but Song of Songs is the Holy of holies."

Q. 48. Preachers often seem to use images from the Song of Songs in new ways. Even Cardinal Newman did it—is this legitimate?

Your question exemplifies another aspect of biblical interpretation: the application of biblical texts to new situations. In the Song the poet has placed on the mouth of the woman a poem describing a visit of the lover who comes "leaping over the hills" to her home where he issues an invitation to a rendezvous: "Arise, my friend, my beautiful one, and come!" This is a propitious time, because the winter is over; it is spring with the rains gone and blossoms appearing. Here the theme of spring is utilized to move the girl to leave her house for a meeting outdoors. She is to experience the newness of life that nature celebrates. Similarly, Cardinal Newman wished to celebrate the newness of life of the Roman Catholic Church in England. The year 1850 marked the restoration of the Roman Catholic hierarchy. Cardinal Newman commemorated the event by a stirring sermon to his community that was entitled "The Second Spring," and the text, of course, was taken from the spring song, Canticle 2:10–12. As the cardinal put it, "The English Church was, and the English Church was not, and the English Church is once again. This is the portent, worthy of a cry. It is the coming in of a Second Spring; it is a restoration in the moral world, such as that which yearly takes place in the physical."

Q. 49. I think I heard part of the Song of Songs read at a wedding ceremony I attended. Can you comment on this?

You heard correctly. Among the several readings from the Old and New Testaments suggested in the Roman ritual for marriage is a reading that combines some verses of the spring song with 8:6. Since I have just mentioned the spring song let me deal in some detail with 8:6

which is surely one of the more important passages in the book. This
verse is spoken by the woman to the man, and I translate it as follows:

> Place me as a seal on your heart,
>   as a seal on your arm.
> Strong as Death is love
>   intense as Sheol is ardor.
> Its shafts are shafts of fire,
>   the flame of Yah.

The comparisons are significant. A seal would be carried always on the
person as a kind of identification card (cf. Gen 38:18). It would be a
small object of stone or metal with writing or a design on it that could
make an impression on clay or wax. All kinds of seals developed over
the years, as might be expected. They could be worn on the arm or
attached to a cord around the neck. The symbol in 8:6 stands for the
closeness of the woman to the man, just as today one might wear a
locket or picture of the beloved. The comparison of love to Death is
carried on in the parallel line where ardor is compared to Sheol. Most
translations have "jealousy" or "passion" instead of "ardor." But the
parallelism favors the latter term; jealousy is not an issue in the Song,
and passion is too easily understood as only the sexual component of
love. The comparison is a tremendous compliment to love. The strength
of Death/Sheol was one of the greatest that the Old Testament person
knew (see Q. 8). It was a dynamic power that pursued all human beings
until it finally claimed them; no one would escape. This is the term of
comparison for the powerful drive of the love between a man and a
woman. Love refuses to give up; the lover pursues the beloved with a
zeal comparable to that of Sheol. It is not that love and death are locked
in struggle; the point of emphasis is rather the quality of love. It reaches
its goal, the beloved, just as Death inevitably does.

The end of verse 6 is also important; it says that the shafts of love
are fiery shafts, and the metaphor is continued in "the flame of Yah."
The last phrase is usually translated as an "intense" flame. The use of
the (short) form of the sacred name, "Yah," is taken as the sign of the
superlative—a god-like or intense flame. This is possible. But a more
literal translation (followed also by the New Jerusalem Bible, "a flame
of Yahweh himself") is also possible and even preferable. Accordingly,

the line could mean that human love resembles the flame of divine love. Just how human love is compared to God's love is not said. It could be for intensity; perhaps even for origin (cf. 1 Jn 4:7–8: "....love is from God....God is love"). If this interpretation is correct, it means that the oft-repeated statement that God is not mentioned in the Song is simply not true. But more important than the mere presence of the sacred name is the connection that is made between human and divine love. Sexual love (admittedly only one aspect of human love) is related to God, whether by way of origin or participation. And people ask (see Q. 45) how it came about that such songs as these were incorporated into the Bible?

RUTH

Q. 50. Is the Book of Ruth history or a short story?

Your question is doubtless prompted by two considerations. The first is the genealogies that occur at the end of the book (Ruth 4:17–22). They focus on David, son of Jesse, and ultimately a descendant of a Moabite woman, Ruth. The historical character of the work is suggested perhaps by the place of the book in the Christian Bible, where it comes after Judges, following the Septuagint and Vulgate order, and also by the setting of the book (1:1, "in the days when the judges ruled, a famine occurred...."). The second reason is the unusual quality of the narrative, which is a literary masterpiece and has more the flavor of a creation than a description of hard reality. The book has only eighty-five verses and of these fifty-five are dialogue. The dialogue certainly accounts for the charm that the book wields. The bare facts are hardly newsworthy. A Bethlehemite family flees famine and goes to Moab where the two young sons marry Moabite women. But when the father and sons die, the widow Naomi is grief-stricken and the family seems destined for oblivion. However, one of the Moabite daughters-in-law, Ruth, refuses to leave Naomi, and they both go to Bethlehem where Ruth is eventually married to Boaz, a local landowner, and a future line is assured by the birth of a child. What secures the story's success is the high noble sentiment, the family qualities of all concerned, and the vivid presentation of the course of events.

Perhaps the narrative can be described as a short story with histori-cal roots. If one grants that there are historical roots, these would be in the Moabite ancestry of David (cf. Ruth 4:17). That is not likely to be an invention. But the marvelous literary quality of the narrative sug-gests a short story.

Q. 51. What do you mean by the "marvelous literary quality" of the work?

By this I don't mean to exclude other qualities, such as the theologi-cal implications. I would like to include the literary and theological together.

From a literary point of view, we should note the slow lingering over important events, and the rapid transitions that carry a reader's interest immediately to the dramatic scenes. Within the first seven verses many years elapse and are marked by marriage and death. Suddenly there is the emotional departure of Naomi for Bethlehem. Three times Naomi generously and gently advises her daughters-in-law not to come with her. They have opportunities to be married in their own homeland (recall that marriage was the desired and accept-able state in life for a woman). They do not wish to leave Ruth. Finally, Orpah will obey, but not Ruth who delivers the beautiful address: "wherever you go, I will go; wherever you lodge, I will lodge; your people shall be my people and your God my God. Where you die, I shall die and be buried there" (1:16–17). This total devotion (in 1:8 Ruth had remarked on their *hesed*, or love) is sealed by an impreca-tion: "Thus and more may the Lord do to me if even death shall sepa-rate me from you." So generosity is met by generosity. Already theological issues have surfaced: the gods of Moab to which Orpah returns and the God of Israel whom Ruth identifies with.

A very quick transition to Bethlehem takes place and the reaction of the local women serves to introduce Naomi's grief, and the theological issue of retribution. She is not to be called "pleasant" (Naomi), but "bitter" (Mara), for God has turned against her (1:21).

Another quick shift is made, this time to a harvest scene where Boaz, a kinsman to the dead husband of Naomi, is introduced as a gentle farmer, who allows Ruth to glean, gathering what is left after the harvesting. In a series of moves he shows extraordinary generosity until she can be treated as one of the maidservants—all this happens after the hint of God's providence in 2:2–3. Ruth tells Naomi she hopes to glean wherever she is permitted, and it just "happens" that this is the field belonging to Naomi's relative. As time goes on, and both Ruth and Boaz prove their valor, Naomi concocts her curious plan to speed up her designs. Ruth spends the night with Boaz—the narrative is extraordinarily discreet—and in the morning Boaz is determined upon marriage.

In an official transaction at the city gate, Boaz obtains from a closer relative to the right to act as *go'el*, or kinsman with the opportunity to acquire inheritance property and to marry Ruth. We are not sure just what law is behind this transaction (it doesn't appear to be Deuteronomy 25:5–10, levirate marriage). In any case, the unknown kinsman yields his claim to Boaz. The marriage of Boaz and Ruth and the birth of a child are quickly narrated. The joyous celebration over the birth of Obed marks the happy turn in Naomi's life (cf. 1:20–21). A genealogical appendix is added in 4:18–22 (cf. 1 Chron 2:9–12), and it orients the entire book toward the question of David's ancestors.

This raises the question of the theology of the work. Although the book emphasizes that there was a Moabite in David's line, this should not be taken as a (post-exilic) objection to the prohibition of mixed marriages found in the books of Ezra-Nehemiah. It is not a tirade or an attack. The gentle pace of the events suggests that it is a story of Providence, a hidden Providence in which God is secretly working. The human elements that make up this narrative have to do with the preservation of the name, and the continuation of the family—these goals are not possible without the love and family loyalty so beautifully described.

QOHELETH

Q. 52. What does the name "Qoheleth" mean? We used to call it Ecclesiastes, didn't we?

This simple question is not easy to answer. First, is the word a proper name? In the Hebrew text it occurs seven times, twice with the definite article. The article would seem to indicate that it was not quite yet a proper name, but perhaps on the way to becoming one. In any case, it is treated as a proper name by modern people. The meaning is also uncertain. We know that the root of the word is *qhl*, which has to do with an assembly or congregation. Hence, one can understand immediately why the Greek and Latin tradition rendered the word as Ecclesiastes (*ecclesia* being a congregation, or church). However, this does not solve the riddle, and other meanings have been proposed. Jerome used the Latin word, *concionator* or speaker, which lies behind the popular "Preacher" in so many English translations (*RSV*, but "Teacher" in *NRSV*). Doubtless the German translation of Martin Luther was also a factor: *Prediger* (this means "preacher"). The idea in this name is also associated with the root meaning of "assemble." The writer is understood to be one who leads an assembly by way of preaching or teaching them.

The most difficult thing to understand is that the name is the feminine participle form of the verb *qhl*, and the author seems to be a male. Perhaps this can be explained by the usage of feminine participles to indicate some kind of office or function, which gradually became a proper name. The analogy to this would be the ancestral names Hassophereth (one who prepares leather) and Pochereth-hazzebaim (one who tends gazelles), that occur in Ezra 2:55–57. But we are really at a loss to explain the form with any certainty.

Q. 53. Isn't this Qoheleth also called "son of David" and "king in Jerusalem"—so he could be Solomon, couldn't he?

You are perfectly right about those titles in the superscription (1:1), but notice that the name of Solomon does not appear, either here or in the rest of the book. The real question is: Why is the author of this book associated with royalty and specifically the "son of David," presumably Solomon? In 1:12 the writer speaks of himself as "I, Qoheleth, was king over Israel in Jerusalem." Moreover, the description of his experiment with pleasure in chapter 2 suggests a monarch who had extensive power over people and possessions, one who flourished "more than all who were before me in Jerusalem" (2:9). Actually Solomon could hardly be said to have had predecessors in Jerusalem. Nonetheless, the emphasis on wisdom in 2:3,9 supports the identity with Solomon. The tradition about Solomon the wise seems to be enough to explain these references. There is a fiction at work in chapter 2—only the rich and wise Solomon could have pulled off this experiment. However, this *is* a fiction. The rest of the book gives evidence that King Solomon could not be the writer. First, the language is clearly late, and is not in the usual style of the pre-exilic period. Second, Qoheleth is identified as a sage who taught the people knowledge (12:9)—hardly the task of Solomon. Third, the self-understanding of the author is not that of a king. He is critical of kingship, as the several observations about injustice demonstrate (e.g., 4:1–2). In other passages (8:2–4; 10:4–6), he speaks of how to deal (warily) with a king rather than with how to rule. No, we can be certain that Qoheleth was not the biblical Solomon, and all the evidence points to his being active in the post-exilic period, *circa* 300.

Q. 54. Was Qoheleth written by one person or many?

A short answer would be that at least 12:9–14, the so-called epilogue, was written by someone other than Qoheleth, because it speaks of him in the third person, whereas he usually speaks in the first person in the book. But this would be a superficial answer to your question. Over the centuries there has been a debate, perhaps not strictly on authorship, but on how many "voices," or contrary points of view, are expressed in the work. When Solomonic authorship was simply accepted, the opposing views were explained by attributing them to Solomon reasoning with himself, or quoting fools with whom he was dialoguing. Such maneuvers were necessary, especially to explain those passages which did not fit orthodox doctrine (e.g., human beings have the same lot as animals, 3:18–21). The idea was advanced that he was impersonating the impious, and emphasis was put on his final words about fearing God and keeping the commandments (12:13). These ancient "solutions" have found an echo in the efforts of modern interpreters. Over the last century several hands have been detected in the book. Verses of a decidedly wisdom nature have been attributed to a sage who added them. Similarly, pious or orthodox observations were taken as the work of one who wished to offset the opinions of Qoheleth that caused some shock. However, the tendency today is to explain the book as a whole (since that is also the way it has been handed down to us), without the easy recourse to unknown glossarists. We tend to employ our standards and background, and understand the work in our own logical way. This means the elimination of certain passages that, it is claimed, Qoheleth could not have written. Hence, they are attributed to a putative writer for whom there is no material evidence. Instead, we must recognize that Qoheleth was a very complex thinker, and we must deal with the book as we have it.

Q. 55. I have heard Qoheleth described as an agnostic and skeptic. Is there truth in these charges? How could his work have entered the Bible?

You have heard correctly. He has been described in this way. Let us look at some of the evidence that is advanced to support the charges.

First, agnosticism. Qoheleth is an agnostic insofar as he affirms that we cannot understand what God is doing in this world. He says this several times:

> Just as you do not know the way of the life-breath
> in the limbs within a mother's womb,
> so you do not know the work of God
> who does everything. (11:5)

The comparison of God's work to the mysteries of gestation and birth is particularly emphatic.

Again, he says, "I looked at all the work of God: no one can find out what is done under the sun. Therefore humans search hard, but no one can find out, and even if the wise man says he knows, he cannot find out" (8:17). The work of God remained a conundrum to Qoheleth: "Who can make straight what he has made crooked?" (7:13; cf. 1:15). And God is responsible for this situation, for God has put something into the heart of human beings—call it duration, the world, or whatever—so that "they cannot find out, from beginning to end, the worker which God has done" (3:11).

Is this type of agnosticism incompatible with faith? No, faith sees mystery and acknowledges it. Human beings recognize the divine at work and "fear" it: "for I know that God has done so that they may stand in awe of him" (3:14). The vaunted "agnosticism" of Qoheleth turns out to be a healthy skepticism.

What kind of skepticism is "healthy"? It is one that recognizes the chasm between the divine and the human. Israel always had this sense, and there are countless testimonies to the mystery of God in the Old Testament ("My ways are not your ways..." Is 55:9; "for the Lord does not see as mortals see..." 1 Sam 16:7). Qoheleth has plumbed the depths of these theological statements, and he was not prevented by a false superficial religiosity to proclaim his view openly. Agnosticism is understood today as just a step below atheism. This understanding simply doesn't do justice to the subtle viewpoint of Qoheleth; it carries too much modern baggage. Skepticism is a more nuanced term that captures his hard-nosed views. It may be objected that at times he takes an unreasonably dim view of reality. For example, he overrates the fact of human death when he is comparing humans and animals. Perhaps it is we who have acquired different standards. Thus, we might willingly endure riches even if their possession cost us some sleep (5:11). If Qoheleth can detect anything wrong in his world, he tends to highlight it, whereas we are inclined to settle for less than perfection. But he certainly refuses to be taken in by the slick claims of his society.

Q. 56. You have mentioned Qoheleth's "faith." How do you define the faith of an Old Testament person?

There are various ways of looking at faith. If we take it as a certain content that one "believes," a common description is found in Deuteronomy 26:5–9. This is an insert into a ritual in which the first fruits of the harvest are offered to God, and the following prayer is found: "My father was a wandering Aramean who went down to Egypt and lived there as an alien. Though few in number he became a great nation, strong and numerous. When the Egyptians maltreated us...we cried to the Lord, the God of our fathers, and he heard our voice. The Lord brought us out of Egypt...into this place and gave us this land...." This is, as it were, the self-understanding of the ancient Israelite. It is a review of the classic period of salvation from Egypt that can be likened to a profession of faith (it has been called "a little credo").

If we look at faith from a more subjective point of view, the psalms give many examples of the reliance, the trust, of the psalmist in the Lord—reliance on God for the goods of this world, for deliverance from adversity, and so on. One is reminded of that description of Paul in Acts 14:9, when Paul looks intently at the cripple in Lystra and saw that he had the faith to be healed. Similarly God answered the faith of the Israelites in many ways.

Qoheleth exemplifies a fundamental aspect of faith which is not often adverted to. It has to do with acceptance and adherence to God. He accepted God on God's terms. These were to him very mysterious, even harsh, terms, but he didn't blink. He accepted. Job rebelled, since that is an aspect which the author of the book wanted to emphasize. There is no *agōn* in Qoheleth, but there is a steely resolve that concentrates on his mysterious God.

Q. 57. Isn't Qoheleth the one who urges us to eat, drink, and be merry?

Yes, at least seven times Qoheleth proffers a conclusion of that sort: 2:24; 3:12–13,22; 5:17–18; 8:15; 9:7–9; 11:8–9. From a material point of view—simply looking at the words—this attitude is reflected and rejected in Isaiah 22:13: "Let us eat and drink, for tomorrow we die." This is a condemnation of revelers (Is 5:11–12) who refuse to change their ways despite the prophet's threats. Qoheleth's views are quite different. He earnestly recommends pleasure, often expressed in the popular merism, "eat and drink." However, he sees such joy as a gift coming from God: 2:24; 3:13; 5:18. But precisely because pleasure is a gift from the mysterious God, one cannot count on it. One never knows if one will lose it (and Qoheleth gives various examples of disaster, as in 5:12; 6:2). God may be lavish with gifts, but possessions can also be an occasion of divine capriciousness.

Qoheleth's attitude has been debated among scholars. Does he deserve to be called a "preacher of joy," or are the divine gifts quite arbitrary? Perhaps a simple yes or no cannot be given to this question, insofar as Qoheleth can change his mind. Thus, in 9:7 he says: "Go, eat your bread with joy and drink your wine with a merry heart because God has already accepted your deeds." Is some kind of divine approval, and more important, divine intention, indicated here? I still think that the mystery of the divine work lies behind 9:7. The gifts freely bestowed are completely at the (arbitrary) will of God; they are not "earned," and humans have no title to them. One never knows if one is winning or losing.

We cannot gloss over the frightening statement of 9:1–2, "Indeed, all this I took to heart, and all this I examined: the just and the wise and their actions are in the hand of God. Love from hatred human beings cannot tell; both are before them. Everything is the same for everybody: the same lot for the just and the wicked...." Qoheleth says here that from the point of view of experience (and this is the viewpoint of wisdom), we cannot determine whether God loves us or hates us. This does not mean that he necessarily denies such traditional biblical statements as in Exodus 34:6, "The Lord, the Lord, a God merciful and gracious...." It is just that experience does not bear this out. Many people might *believe* this. But as 9:1 would put it, you cannot tell whether God loves you or hates you by the way that God treats you. Belief is one thing and experience is another, and experience may seem to contradict it often.

With this background let us look again at the question. Yes, Qoheleth encourages us to rejoice in our lives, *if* things turn out in our favor. But we can have no certainty about this. Therefore, God can only be said to be arbitrary in providing such opportunities. God gives them to whom she will. This was also clear from the beginning, if one recalls that famous text from Exodus 33:19, "I will be gracious to whom I will be gracious, and I will show mercy on whom I will show mercy." One can only see the recommendations of Qoheleth as very limited encouragement. If joy and pleasure come your way, take advantage of it—but you can neither expect it nor possess it with any certainty. It is a sort of "resigned" conclusion—the best that Qoheleth has to offer.

Q. 58. What does "vanity of vanities" mean?

The duplication of the same word is, of course, the Hebrew idiom for the superlative, like "Song of Songs," or "King of Kings." The importance of the phrase is that it is the inclusion or envelope for the book, occurring at 1:2 and 12:8. The Hebrew word, *hebel*, occurs thirty-eight times in the book, and that is over half of the number of times it occurs in the entire Bible. It has a basic meaning of vapor or breath, and from this other meanings are derived: fleeting (human life), vain and ineffectual, and even deceitful (such as idols that cannot really satisfy a worshipper). Hence *hebel* is often rendered by futile, worthless, and even absurd (at least in the sense of incomprehensible, unknowable). A course of action or an event can be considered *hebel* because it makes no sense, by human judgment.

The common English translation, "vanity," is really not strong enough for the term as used by Qoheleth. In English "vain" lacks the impact of futile or absurd. Hence, there may be a temptation to overlook the seriousness with which Qoheleth uses the word. He pronounces the verdict of *hebel* upon many actions and values, and he means it seriously. We might settle for less and not be impressed with his judgment. But it is his judgment that counts, and he obviously considered life in general as rather hopeless. Some would counter this by pointing to his use of the saying, "a live dog is better off than a dead lion." Hence he offers hope to the living (9:4). But he goes on to say the dead know nothing while the living at least know something, and what is that? That they will die!

Q. 59. Death never seemed to pose a problem in the Old Testament; it was simply accepted with resignation. Why is Qoheleth so opposed to such resignation?

You are quite correct about the Old Testament view of death. There is a remarkable resignation to the fact of human mortality, and to the reality of Sheol, which is described by Qoheleth with these words: "There is no action, or answer, or knowledge, or wisdom in Sheol where you are going" (9:10). Death was simply accepted as the lot of human beings: "We must all die; we are like water poured out on the ground that cannot be gathered up" (2 Sam 14:14). It was made easier by the mere fact of a lengthy and full life. Old age was a sign of God's blessing for virtue. The problem of premature death was a puzzle, unless it happened to evil people; they deserved such a fate. More weighty than physical death was the dynamic concept of Death and Sheol, which were conceived to be powers that irrupted into human life (see Q. 8). And we have seen that in the case of Job, Death/Sheol could be wished for as a place of respite from suffering in this world (Job 3:21–22; 7:15; 14:13).

But Qoheleth is totally dissatisfied with human mortality. While he is generally very sober and matter-of-fact, one can hear the plaintive cry in 2:16, "How can the wise die just like the fools?" There should be some distinction! But there is not even a differentiation between humans and animals: "As one dies, so does the other; both have the same life-breath. Both go to the same place; both are from the dust and both return to the dust" (3:19–20). It appears that in his day some people were trying to make a distinction, but he denies this: "Who knows if the life-breath of humans goes upwards, and if the life-breath of animals goes down into the earth?" (3:21). Hence, there is no doctrine of immortality in Ecclesiastes 12:7, which speaks of the spirit returning to God who gave it. This does not refer to the soul; it refers to the life-breath that God bestows on living things, and is taken back.

Q. 60. Qoheleth mentions fear of God. Was he a God-fearer, in view of all the things he says about God?

The concept of the fear of God, as one might expect, is to be found throughout the Hebrew Bible. Its meaning depends on the various contexts in which it is found. In the episode of the burning bush, Moses hides his face, for he "feared" to look on God. This fear of beholding God (lest one would die) stems from a deep sense of awe before the powerful divinity, who is so totally other than human. In current English usage, "fear" is too often understood and dismissed as servile fear (one thinks of the way the Satan seems to have interpreted the fear of God that Job had; Job 1:1,9). But biblical nuances are very rich. One can easily understand how Israel is overcome by fear in the theophany of Exodus 20:15–18. Moses assures the people that this is God testing them, inspiring awe or fear, so that they will keep from doing wrong. This is in striking contrast to the many texts in Deuteronomy (e.g., 8:6; 10:12, 20) where fear, love and obedience to God are taken almost synonymously. The faithful (an individual or the community) in the psalms is also one who fears God. In Ben Sira (e.g., Sir 1:11–20), the fear of God is a key theme in his work. This is not surprising in the wisdom literature. In the book of Proverbs fear of the Lord serves as a kind of motto in 1:7 (see also 9:10; 15:33; Job 28:28; Ps 111:10)—the beginning of wisdom is fear of the Lord.

Qoheleth does not use the phrase "fear of God/Lord." He uses the verbal form, "to fear" (God). In 3:14 he describes God as acting so that humans will fear (i.e., stand in awe of). This is not a comforting view, since we have already seen that it is impossible to understand the divine action. In 5:6 he warns against verbosity and rashness in prayer to God; he begins this warning with the command, "Fear God!" that is surely in the spirit of Moses and the prophets. But in 8:12 we come upon a statement in which he seems to contradict himself: "I know that those who fear God will be well off because they fear him, and that the wicked person will not be well off, and will not prolong his shadowy days because he does not fear God." This is one of those verses that many interpreters attribute to someone other than Qoheleth, and it is easy to see why. It does not fit with his denial of justice for the righteous and punishment for the wicked (cf. 8:11–12a). However, this statement in 8:12 introduced by the words, "for also I know." These introductory words seem to indicate that Qoheleth is quoting the common theory of divine retribution which distinguished between the righteous and the wicked. He knows this is what the orthodox theory upholds, but it does not square with reality. In the first part of 8:12 he has already said that the sinner does evil a hundred times and yet prolongs his life—and there are other statements to the same effect. So Qoheleth, like Job, clearly rejected the accepted theory of retribution (e.g., 8:14; 9:2). The problem is to square 8:12–13 with his general position. I would argue that he says he knows the prevailing theory of divine justice—but he also knows that it doesn't work.

The fear of God also occurs in the epilogue (12:9–14), which is generally considered to be due to the hand of an editor (see Q. 63). Verse 13 puts it this way: "Fear God and keep the commandments." It is the union of the two ideas that is the problem. Qoheleth is not against fearing God, nor is he opposed to the observance of the commandments. But it is the way that these two admonitions are joined together that catches our attention. Singly, they are in line with the teaching of the book. But together they suggest that virtuous conduct will be rewarded by God. It gives a tilt to the final words that is very unlike Qoheleth's general stance. He never speaks of the commandments, and it would be far from his thought to suggest that observance of the commandments brought security in this life; there is no infallible means to security.

Q. 61. What does Qoheleth mean by saying that one who digs a pit will fall into it (10:8)?

Falling into a pit one has dug is a frequent image in the Bible. It generally means that the one who digs a pit for another party to fall into suffers the accident and the other party is left unharmed. Today we speak of "poetic justice," when a person who intends harm in the end suffers that very harm. The image in Psalm 7:15–16 (cf. also 9:16b) describes the activity of the wicked:

> They make a pit, digging it out,
> and fall into the hole that they have made.
> Their mischief returns upon their own heads,
> and on their own heads their violence descends. (*NRSV*)

The same idea is found in Proverbs 26:27, where the context is condemning the evil which the wicked perpetrate:

> Whoever digs a pit falls into it,
> and a stone comes back on whoever rolls it.

These popular sayings could be illustrated in Israel's tradition: In Esther 7:10 Haman is hanged on the gibbet that he planned for Mordecai. Those who accused Daniel to King Darius are themselves thrown into the lions' den that was prepared for Daniel (Dan 6:7,24).

Now, is this an ironclad rule? Does every evil deed planned against an innocent person have a boomerang effect upon the wicked instigator? Obviously not. The truth of the saying lay in the fitness, not the frequency, of it. It would not have taken much time or thought to realize that such happenings were not frequent—much less automatic. Wrongdoing is not so easily requited. Indeed, one may surmise that it was the rarity that caught the popular imagination and gave rise to the saying. As Shakespeare might put it, the wicked was hoist on his own petard.

The saying of Ecclesiastes 10:8 is taken as an example of the "act-consequence" mentality. Many scholars have asserted that ancient Israel lived by this rule: good begets good and evil begets evil. This is, as it were, an order that God implanted in the universe and over which the divinity watched. Scholars go on to say that this rule of order was seen to be bankrupt by the authors of Job and Ecclesiastes, and hence came the "crisis" or downfall of wisdom. Such a scenario is simply wrong-headed. There are as many times in the Bible in which God is portrayed as taking a *direct* hand in affairs. It may very well be that this "act-consequence" mentality functioned along with the idea that God directly intervened. But it was not the axis of wisdom thought.

Let us return to Ecclesiastes 10:8. Verses 8 and 9 are usually translated thus:

> Whoever digs a pit will fall into it;
>   and whoever breaks through a well will be bitten by a snake.
> Whoever quarries stone will be hurt by them;
>   and whoever splits logs will be endangered by them. (*NRSV*)

I submit that the translation of the main verbs is not exact. The Hebrew form can be taken as modal, rather than factual; hence "may fall" or "may be bitten"; "may be hurt" or "may be endangered." A very misleading idea is given by the indicative mood. The consideration of the examples are enough to prove that. One is not always hurt by quarrying or by log-splitting. And how often was the ancient Palestinian bitten by a snake (which admittedly could nestle in the loose fill of the rocks of private houses; cf. Amos 5:19)? Rather, this is a series of observations that illustrate the uncertainties and the unexpected in the affairs of life. Accidents *do* happen, and one must be on one's guard. The context of these verses is against their being understood as factual examples of a mechanical sequence of act and consequence.

Q. 62. Was Qoheleth a male chauvinist?

It would not be surprising if he were, and the majority of interpreters claim that he was. But a substantial minority questions the translation of the text which forms the basis for the charge. I say that it would not be surprising, because the attitude of men toward women in the Hellenistic world (and in the Semitic world generally) was very harsh.

The text in question is 7:25-29. Qoheleth begins with an announcement of his intent to investigate wisdom (v 25; cf. 1:17; 2:12; 8:16), and he takes up the topos of a particular type of woman in v 26, whom he has "found more bitter than death." This is the one who is described as a snare (as in Prov 6:25, the same word is used of the "strange woman"). There can hardly be any doubt that Qoheleth is following the typical warning of the sages (cf. Prov, chaps. 5–7) in warning against sexual involvement. Then his style becomes exceedingly repetitive and complicated. The usual translation runs this way: "See, this is what I found, says the Teacher, adding one thing to another to find the sum, which my mind has sought repeatedly, but I have not found. One man among a thousand I found, but a woman among all these I have not found. See, this alone I found, that God made human beings straightforward, but they have devised many schemes" (vv 26–29, *NRSV*).

In this translation Qoheleth seems to say that he could not find a woman in a thousand although he found one man. The presumption is that he is talking about an upright person (and one in a thousand is hardly complimentary to males!). But I think the translation should go this way: "Indeed, this I have found—says Qoheleth, adding one thing to another to find an answer—what my soul has always sought, without finding (is this): One man in a thousand I have found, but a woman among all of these I have not found." In other words, I think Qoheleth is *denying* the saying about one in a thousand. One cannot find even one male, much less a female! And why? The last verse (v 29) says they are all at fault: "See, only this I have found: God made humans upright, but they have sought out many devices." Now verse 29 makes sense: both male and female are blameworthy. It would make no sense to regard males as somehow superior (one in a thousand) in verse 28, and then to say that human beings across the board are devious, although God made them upright. Therefore, I would argue that you cannot claim that Qoheleth was a misogynist on the basis of this notorious text in 7:25–29, which is usually interpreted that way.

I would not deny that Qoheleth shared the patriarchal bias of a male-centered society. It was all too easy for males to be bigoted on this score (e.g., cf. Sir 25:13–26, and in contrast, 36:27–31, although this passage is marred by the judgment in 36:26).

Q. 63. Isn't the epilogue to the book (Eccl 12:9–14) a putdown of Qoheleth?

Many commentators think that it is. How would you like to write a book that ended with a line like 12:12, "...beware, there is no end to the writing of many books, and much study wearies the flesh"? It is certainly not an encouragement to write, or even to read any more! But this epilogue deserves more careful analysis than simply picking out a verse.

First, there is general agreement that 12:9–14 is a later addition to the book. It speaks of the author in the third person, *about* Qoheleth, in contrast to the first person style which characterizes the rest of the book. Second, it characterizes Qoheleth in a manner that is personal and unlike the reticence he chooses to exercise. Thus we are told that he was a sage (*hakam*) who taught the people knowledge. His goal was the analysis of the tradition of sapiential sayings (*měshalim*). These he subjected, as we have seen, to rigorous examination. When 12:10 tells us that he "sought to find out pleasing words," the meaning is that his writing would be well-turned, attractive, the kind of subtle language that is characteristic of the literature of the sages. The writer of the epilogue goes on to praise the wisdom writings: "The words of the wise are like oxgoads, like fixed nails,..." The rest of his statement is difficult to understand but it is in a complimentary mode. It is then that he says: "As for more than these, my son, beware...." and we have the saying about many books which was quoted above. Is this to be understood as a negative judgment on Qoheleth? Rather, the opposite. He seems to be saying that since we now have the book of Ecclesiastes, we need no more books of wisdom. This is a compliment to the book of Ecclesiastes which is, as it were, the height of wisdom. For study and writing are a difficult task. It is as if the writer said: We have enough now with the book to which this epilogue is being added.

But the epilogue is not over. We read in verses 13–14 that, "The end of the matter, when all is heard, is: fear God and keep his commandments for this is the duty of everyone. For God will bring every deed to judgment, over all that is hidden, whether good or evil." Are these verses hostile to Qoheleth's teaching? Many commentators think they were added to ease the way for Ecclesiastes into the list of accepted and eventually "canonical" books. This could hardly achieve so formidable a goal. If the author of the epilogue was really serious about "sanitizing" the work and making it pleasing to "religious" people, he was woefully negligent. He could have edited the work so as to drop the seemingly unorthodox statements of Qoheleth. No, this is not an effort to manipulate the work. It is true, as mentioned in Q. 60, that these verses give a certain slant to the book that differs from that of Qoheleth. It has been said that it is the kind of viewpoint that flourished in the time of Ben Sira (circa 200). This fact is significant for the impact of Qoheleth's work. It was not regarded as "shocking," but seen in the light of the total wisdom movement (see Q. 65). Therefore, I would answer your question in the negative, and claim that 12:12, in particular, is laudatory, and not a putdown.

Q. 64. How has the book of Qoheleth been received by Jews and Christians?

Obviously the book is in both the Hebrew and the Christian Bibles, and hence enjoys that dignity. However, it has had an interesting history of interpretation.

In the Jewish tradition, it raised questions. Apparently after it was already in the official books of the Jews—those holy books that "soiled the hands," as they put it—some objections were made. But they were satisfactorily handled by various considerations, especially Solomonic authorship. For example, the Targum thought that Solomon foresaw the sad history of Israel down to the exile, and that he recognized the failure of his son Rehoboam. The futility of which "Solomon" writes is due to this sad history, and also to the fact that he was deposed from the throne, according to legend. A more important factor was the Torah, or law. It has been pointed out that the biblical wisdom books did not attract much attention in the rabbinic period (from about 70 to 640). Qoheleth came to be viewed in the light of the law. The "profit" about which he so often wrote lay in the study of the law. There is a very interesting passage in the Talmud (b. *Shabbat*, 30b) that indicates how the epilogue figured in all this:

> The Sages wished to hide the Book of Ecclesiastes, because its words are self-contradictory, yet why did they not hide it? Because its beginning is religious teaching and its end is religious teaching,

as it is written, *What profit had man of all his labour wherein he laboreth under the sun?* And the School of R. Janna commented: Under the sun he has none, but he has it (*sc.* profit) before the sun. The end thereof is religious teaching, as it is written, *Let us hear the conclusion of the matter, fear God and keep his commandments: for this is the whole of man.* What is meant by, *"for this is the whole of man"?*—Said R. Eleazar. The entire world was created only for the sake of this (type of) man. Simeon b. 'Azzai— others state, Simeon b. Zoma—said: The entire world was created only to be a companion to this man.

It is ironic that the epilogue, which was seen as favorable to Qoheleth in Jewish tradition, has been interpreted so unfavorably by modern commentators.

As with the Jews, Solomonic authorship counted importantly for Christians. But the motto of the book, "vanity of vanities" (1:2; 12:8) served to underline many Christian values. Belief in immortality, a life with God beyond this one, made this world and its values appear vain indeed. St. Jerome was the most influential commentator. He wrote his commentary around A.D. 339 for a certain Blesilla. When he was in Rome, he promised a commentary that would motivate her to contempt of the world. She died before he could write his work (in Bethlehem) but his emphasis on the ascetical values dominated later Christian exegesis. This is particularly evident as late as Thomas à Kempis, who writes at the beginning of his *Imitation of Christ,* "'vanity of vanities, all is vanity,' unless we serve God and love him with our whole heart (*Eccles* 1, 2). Oh, this is the highest and safest wisdom, that by contempt of the world we endeavor to please God." Obviously, this is a misreading of the total message of the book. Eschatological belief can distort a proper evaluation of God's creation.

Q. 65. You say that Qoheleth belongs to the wisdom tradition, but isn't he really "anti-wisdom"?

I think that the term "anti-wisdom" is too vague and does not do justice to the views of Qoheleth. We might review the facts.

First, this judgment is often made by those who count only three wisdom books: Proverbs, Job, and Ecclesiastes, and the contrast between the first and the following two is perhaps enough for them to make their own allegation. But these three books, it should be remembered, were followed by Sirach (Ecclesiasticus) and the Wisdom of Solomon. When one takes this broader look at wisdom, a better judgment is possible. What I mean is that Sirach is closer in doctrine to Proverbs than to Job or to Ecclesiastes. The wisdom movement did not end with Ecclesiastes. Similarly, the Wisdom of Solomon, written in Greek by a Diaspora Jew (perhaps in Alexandria) exalts wisdom as God's particular possession, but shared with humankind (chaps. 7–9). The point is that the wisdom movement continued and developed, and a new approach to retribution was put forth in the Wisdom of Solomon (cf. R. E. Murphy, *The Tree of Life*, 86–88).

Second, the unfavorable judgment most often coincides with a failure to perceive the intentions of the sages, especially as their wisdom is manifested in the book of Proverbs. The sayings in this book are far from naive. It is true that Proverbs puts forward a decidedly optimistic view of retribution: wisdom or virtue brings prosperity and folly brings destruction (see Q. 21). However, it also points out that there are limitations to wisdom. Of course, Job and Ecclesiastes are more emphatic in pointing out such limitations. But that doesn't mean they are "anti-wisdom." They deal mainly with the problem of retribution—and neither of them answers it, while they both reject the optimism of Proverbs.

Third, Qoheleth himself explicitly states (7:23–24) that wisdom was his goal: "I said, 'I will become wise.' But it was beyond me. What happens is distant and very deep. Who can find it out?" Even though he judged that he failed, he had higher standards than other sages. He refused to be satisfied with easier answers. He is not above jabbing at the traditional wisdom that others took pride in:

> "The wise have eyes in their head,
> but fools walk in darkness."

But I knew also that the same lot comes to them both. So I said to myself: the lot of the fool also comes to me, so why should I be so very wise? Then I said to myself that this also is vanity (2:14–15).

In this dialogue with wisdom he was realistic. He perceived the short-comings of optimism and security, and boldly quarreled with the tradition—in the name of wisdom. Fourth, he was not satisfied with a corpus of teachings. Rather, he attended to the style, the method of wisdom which employed experience and analysis in the assessment of life. Even in conflict with the doctrine, he never abandoned the methodology of the sage. He frequently referred to acting "with wisdom" (2:3,9). He envisioned wisdom directly, but also by its opposites, madness and folly (1:17; 2:12; 7:25).

Fifth, folly is never an option with Qoheleth, and seems to be explicitly rejected in the sayings of 10:2–3. Even a little folly was inexcusable, because wisdom was so vulnerable (9:17–10:1). There was one point in the classical doctrine with which he totally agreed: the condemnation of verbiage, verbosity (cf. Prov 10:19, 21;—the fool talks on and on—Eccl 10:12–14).

Instead of rejecting wisdom, Qoheleth purified it and led it on to greater heights.

ESTHER

Q. 66. How can one determine whether the book of Esther is story or history?

This question could be directed at many other books of the Bible, and each case is different. First, we must clarify our own notions of history. It would be an illusion if we were to expect to find in the Bible history as we define this genre today. The tools and the goals of the modern historian are quite different from the methods employed by the ancients. It is a question of oranges and apples. The "history" that is found in the so-called Deuteronomistic history (Joshua to Kings) is not in the genre of history that we are accustomed to. That does not mean we should abandon the term history for these books. It is just that we must be realistic in our expectations of the ancients. In all likelihood our question 66 would not really have made sense to them; they did not operate with the distinctions that we do. Nevertheless, second, we moderns should be forced to give reasons for discerning one kind of literature from another. Thus it is legitimate for us to ask for indications which clearly place a narrative, or parts of a narrative, outside of the historical genre. Many, perhaps, would not even allow this question 66. Why? Because everything in the Bible is supposed to be "historical." The presupposition behind this statement is that the only truth is history. If it is not history, it is erroneous and cannot be found in the word of God. The mistake that is made is the univocal identification of truth with history. There are many kinds of truth: the truth of a parable (as in the New Testament parables), the truth of a psalm or a love poem, and the truth of a story. Truth is closely connected with the genre of the narrative, and we must make a human (and therefore fallible) judgment about the kind of genre we are dealing with.

It will be helpful to give a very brief summary of the plot of Esther. When Esther replaces Vashti as the queen of King Xerxes (Ahasuerus) of Persia, she is put in a position to thwart the evil plans that Haman makes to destroy the Jewish people in the kingdom. The tables are turned; Esther and her uncle Mordecai become the saviors, while Haman and the enemies of the Jews are defeated. There is nothing implausible in this brief summary; the book might reflect an historical pogrom in the Persian period. It is the details in the story that give us the tipoff that the literary type is not history but something else. Usually the implausibilities in the narrative argue against history.

Thus, the ages of Mordecai and Esther cannot be realistic. According to Esther 2:6 Mordecai was taken into exile in 597, and Xerxes did not reign till over a hundred years later, 486–65. There are signs that the author is exaggerating to make points, and is not interested in recording strict history: the sumptuous feast of 180 days (1:1–3); the implausibility of a royal letter that ordered men to be masters in their own homes (1:22), as if Vashti's disobedience would have such an upsetting effect; the granting of royal permission for the slaughter and plunder of a people within the empire on a year's notice (3:8–15). The abrupt reversal of this decree by the king who seems to be oblivious (despite 3:10–11) of what he previously authorized, seems to mean that anarchy is authorized by royal decree!

We must also examine the way in which the narrative progresses. First we may note that one-fourth of the events are expressed in dialogue (and there were no public media in those days!). The king especially seems to be a dolt, whom the author makes use of in order to raise questions and move the story forward; the king is unaware of Esther's religious identity, and of the fact that Haman is the approved agent for the slaughter of the Jews (7:2–6). The theme of ignorance is essential to the story: Haman must remain ignorant of Esther's Jewish identity and relationship to Mordecai, whom he considers his mortal enemy. The theme is particularly effective in chapter 6, where Haman comes to the king to secure the purpose of hanging Mordecai, ignorant of the fact that the king has plans to honor Mordecai. Again, in chapter 7 Haman is at a sumptuous banquet where Esther will reveal that she is a Jew, and Haman's actions will be misinterpreted by the king. Along with this, the principle of delay functions. Thus Haman becomes aware of Esther's identity when it is too late (7:5–6). Esther delays the dinner appointment she makes with the king and Haman, and postpones it for no apparent reason to the next day.

The story is built up by means of sharp contrasts between characters and events. Mordecai is a descendant of Kish, the father of Saul, and Haman is an Agagite, and thus linked to the Amalekites (3:1; 1 Sam 15:32), with whom Saul did battle. One gets the impression that these two figures are deliberate typification of old hostilities. Once more, Israel will triumph. Mordecai will replace Haman as head of state, while Haman will replace Mordecai on the gallows he has erected especially for Mordecai. Haman feasts while Mordecai fasts (3:15–4:1). There is a remarkable contrast between the words of Zeresh, wife of Haman, in 5:14 and 6:13. One could go on to point out further coincidences and implausibilities within the work, but these are sufficient. There are enough of them to convince us that we are dealing with a carefully constructed story. There are simply too many implausible coincidences to justify the claim for a historical narrative. All the maneuvering within the story are literary flourishes that make sense when we ask ourselves what the point of the author is.

Q. 67. What do you consider is the point of the book of Esther?

There are at least two separate considerations involved in your query. One purpose of the book is to explain the feast of Purim, why it came to be one of the Jewish feasts, although it had no outstanding warrant, such as the Torah, in its favor. Whatever be the true historical origins of the feast, the biblical explanation is given in 3:7 and 9:20–28, 29–32. The word seems to be derived from an Akkadian word for "lot" (*pur* is interpreted in 3:7 by the Hebrew word for "lot," *goral*). The plural form is *purim*. In 3:7 the word is introduced in the story when the lot is cast to determine the month (Adar) in which the Jews were to be slaughtered. Outside of this explanation all kinds of hypotheses concerning Purim have been advanced, e.g., that it was a pagan feast, and only later adopted by the Jews and given a new twist, and so forth.

Another purpose is offered by Professor Brevard Childs (*Introduction to the Old Testament as Scripture* [Philadelphia: Fortress, 1979] 604–07). We must recall the checkered career of the people of God, and the many times their existence was threatened in antiquity as well as in the pogroms of the Christian era. Here we have a worldly, secular story, that while it underlines a providential escape for the people, does not mention the name of God (but cf. 4:14), is also vindictive and reminiscent of the law of an eye for an eye and even more revenge (cf. 9:13–15). Childs points to the significance of 9:20–32. The celebration of Purim that is ordered by Mordecai is "set in the framework of fasting and mourning, the full religious meaning of which has been carefully defined throughout the rest of Israel's sacred tradition. The manner of the celebration in all its original 'secularity' is unchanged, but the object of the hilarity is redefined. All Israel shares in the joy of rest and relief which is dramatized by the giving of gifts, especially to the poor. It is a time to remember by hearing again the story of Purim" (pp. 604–05). The thrust of these verses "draws Purim within the orbit of Israel's religious traditions."

Perhaps the real point of the book for Christians of the twentieth century is the presentation of a pogrom of the Jewish people throughout the Persian empire. They are delivered from it, as they were from slavery in Egypt. But how many shameful pogroms have been inflicted upon them, and by Christians! The book of Esther is there for Christians as well as Jews, and it carries a different message for the persecutors than it does for the persecuted—one of condemnation.

Q. 68. You have said that God is not mentioned in the book of Esther, but then why do we hear readings from Esther in the liturgy where God is mentioned?

You have heard correctly. What you have heard, however, is from the deuterocanonical parts of the book, the so-called Greek Esther. The

Septuagint translation had some six sections, numbered now from A to F. St. Jerome simply packed them in at the end of the Vulgate translation of Esther. When Stephen Langton (d. 1228) divided the Bible into chapters they were simply numbered consecutively, so that the Vulgate has sixteen chapters. But in modern translations, such as the *NAB*, they are inserted in their proper order (although marked as A, B, etc.). The *NRSV* carries these parts, also numbered and alphabetized, in the Apocrypha section of the translation.

You will recall that the term deuterocanonical designates those biblical books or parts of books, whose inspiration was questioned early on, but the matter was settled for Roman Catholics in the Council of Trent. These books, or parts, have the same inspired character as the rest of the Bible. The difference between the Hebrew and the Greek Esther is that the latter has 107 more verses, and God is explicitly mentioned in them. However, I think that God is indicated, although not by name, by Mordecai in Esther 4:14 when he warns her that if she does not act, "relief and deliverance will come to the Jews from another place, but you and your father's family will perish." I think these words can only refer to a deliverance by divine providence, even if God is not explicitly mentioned. The absence of the name seems deliberate, whatever be the reason.

But there is no reticence about the divine name in the Greek Esther; "Lord" or "God" occur more than fifty times. In connection with the passage I just mentioned about help from another place (4:14), Mordecai is quite explicit in 4:9, "Invoke the Lord and speak to the king for us; save us from death." As one would expect, the prayers of Mordecai (C, chap. 13) and Esther (C, chap. 14) are filled with references to the Lord. Mordecai explains his refusal to honor Haman, and begs the Lord's mercy for the people; Esther also prays for the people, and especially because of the danger that threatens her if she comes unbidden before King Xerxes. In general, the additions add to the drama of the narrative and give a clearly religious slant to the development of the events, underlining divine providence, and Esther's fidelity to the law, although married to a gentile king. In the final addition (F, chap. 10) Mordecai interprets the dream with which the Greek Esther began and reinterprets the "lot" of 3:7 and speaks of the two lots made by God: "For this purpose he made arranged two lots: one for the people of God, the second for all the other nations. These two lots were fulfilled in the hour, the time, and the day of judgment before God and among all the nations" (10:7–8, *NAB*). We should recall here that significant proverb: "When the lot is cast into the lap, its decision depends entirely on the Lord" (Prov 16:33).

Q. 69. Isn't the book of Esther a rather bloodthirsty story?

Insofar as it deals with pogrom, I suppose it is. But one must also remember that the story never happened the way it was told. Consider the manner in which the king appears to be the tool of his advisers. When Vashti disobeys the king, the royal counselor, Memucan, orders that the unchangeable royal edict be sent out that Vashti be deposed lest the women of the realm look upon their husbands with contempt— a rather preposterous motive (1:16–22). Then the manic King Xerxes issues an edict at Haman's instigation to wipe out all the Jews in the kingdom. When Esther's Jewish identity is revealed and along with it her probable death, the king is taken aback and seems unaware of Haman's role (7:2–5). Since the laws of the Medes and Persians are "irrevocable" according to the story, a new edict has to be issued. This authorizes the Jews to fight against their would-be murderers on the very day appointed for their own slaughter, the 13th of Adar. Thus anarchy is officially approved by the monarch! By this time the reader can hardly take seriously Esther's proposal to "do it again" in the capital city of Susa. But since a new edict is required, the king conveniently issues one for the city of Susa (9:14–15).

Just what is going on? The maneuver of Esther is dictated by the differing dates of Purim; it explains why there was a difference in the commemoration of the events in Susa and in the rest of the empire. The events transpired on the 13th and 14th, so the celebration of the feast of Purim occurred on the 15th in Susa, whereas in the country there is one day of battle, the 13th, and the celebration was on the 14th of Adar. H. L. Ginsberg remarks, "It is notable that both in the provinces and in Shushan the day of rejoicing is the day that followed the victory, not the day of the victory itself. The explanation of this seems to be that the annual day of rejoicing originally used to be preceded by a mock combat between 'our side' and 'theirs,' much like other such celebrations which are attested in Iran in various ages (and such as were common in Europe down to the preceding century), and that its connection with the deliverance of the Jews from the danger of a pogrom was secondary. The provinces were content with one day of such 'battles,' the self-indulging people of the metropolis observed two. Then, after the daytime 'victory,' nightfall, which—as still in the Jewish calendar—began a new day, ushered in a twenty-four hour period of feasting" (*The Five Megilloth and Jonah* [Philadelphia: Jewish Publication Society, 1969] 87).

The feast of Purim is mentioned in 2 Maccabees 15:36, as "the day of Mordecai." The Greek translation of the book is attributed to a certain Lysimachus of Jerusalem, and the colophon (or ending) to the Greek text also states that it was brought to Egypt in the fourth year of the reign of Ptolemy and Cleopatra, about 78–77 B.C. The feast of Purim became popular in Judaism as a day of exchanging gifts with friends, and giving alms to the poor. As Ginsberg remarks, "the Book of Esther may be described, if one stretches a point or two, as a mock-learned disquisition to be read as the opening of a carnival-like celebration" (p. 83). Hence, many Jewish customs arose, such as making noise with feet or some instrument at the name of Haman whenever it is read—and of playing a game of chance with a top, and also masquerading. Thus it became a joyous feast, despite the threat of annihilation that clung to the book.

Perhaps I have not really answered your question. I have put the bloodshed in a certain context, but I haven't denied it. However, we must not have unreal expectations about the Bible. When one considers the bloodshed of our own era, the "ethnic cleansing" that goes on, the Bible simply narrates human reality. It is true that many have registered shock at the events in the book of Esther. Martin Luther is reported to have said that he could wish it never existed. But opinions can differ. It is said that the great Moses Maimonides (d. 1204) considered the book second to the Torah.

LAMENTATIONS

Q. 70. Do the words lament and lamentation mean the same thing?

In English they can be used interchangeably, but it is better to distinguish them when speaking about the Bible. As we have seen in Q. 5, the "lament" is a particular type of psalm with special structure and characteristics. Lamentation is the term that is used in the title of the book of Lamentations. While in some respects these five chapters can be considered the laments of the community over the fall of Jerusalem, they have a distinctive character. Hence they deserve the nomenclature that has been given to them in antiquity. In Hebrew they are named from the first word, *'êkāh* (literally, "how"; rendered by "Alas," in *NJV*); *thrēnoi* in Greek; *Threni* or *Lamentationes* in Latin.

It should be noted that the book is placed after Ruth in the *megilloth* of the Jewish tradition. In the Christian sequence, it is to be found after the book of Jeremiah to whom the book has been attributed. There may be several reasons for this ascription. We read in Jeremiah 14:17, "Speak to them this word:

> Let my eyes stream with tears
>   day and night, without rest,
> Over the great destruction which overwhelms
>   the virgin daughter of my people,
>   over her incurable wound (*NAB*).

Passages like these suggest an affinity between Lamentations and this prophet who could write:

> Oh, that my head were a spring of water,
>   my eyes a fountain of tears,
> That I might weep day and night
>   over the slain of the daughter of my people (8:23, *NAB*).

It has also been pointed out that according to 2 Chronicles 35:25–26 there was a great mourning when King Josiah was slain at Megiddo in 609, and "Jeremiah also composed a lamentation over Josiah, which is recited to this day by all the male and female singers in their lamentations over Josiah. These have been made obligatory for Israel, and can be found written in the Lamentations" (*NAB*). Contrary to the footnote in the *NAB*, the reference to the canonical book of Lamentations is *not* probable. The canonical book has nothing to do with Josiah. This reference may have contributed to the reputed authorship of Lamentations by Jeremiah. But the fact of the matter is that the author—whether one or many—is simply unknown.

Q. 71. Wouldn't one expect these five chapters to have been included in the book of Psalms?

That is surely a possibility, and one cannot really give a complete answer to your question. However, the following peculiarities of the work might be noted.

First, there is the liturgical occasion on which the lamentations were recited. At the present time they are prayed on the anniversary of the destruction of Jerusalem (the ninth of Ab). These prayers seem to have crystallized around a liturgical commemoration. One is reminded of the event related in Jeremiah 41:5 (see also Zech 7:1–5; 8:18–19), where it is related that "eighty men with beards shaved off, clothes in rags, and with gashes on their bodies, came from Shechem, Shiloh and Samaria, bringing food offerings and incense for the house of the Lord." It is worthy of note that they came just after the destruction of Jerusalem from the old northern kingdom, that their mourning is genuine, that they feel obliged to make a pilgrimage to the Temple. Due to the lawless condition of the times, their mission was disastrous—but that is beside the point. The incident shows the attachment of people to the sanctuary, almost immediately after Jerusalem had been destroyed.

Second, the poems (except chap. 5) have a very peculiar style, varying from the usual parallelism that characterizes the psalms and Hebrew poetry. It does have a rhythm, called the *qinah*, that consists in three stresses or accents, followed by two stresses or accents. For example, 1:2,

> Bitterly she-weeps at-night,
> tears upon-her-cheeks.

This 3 + 2 meter is not typical of all laments, but it is found frequently in this book, and gives it a certain character.

Third, there is an interesting and varied use of the acrostic pattern. In chapters 1 and 2 there are 22 (the number of letters in the Hebrew alphabet) stanzas, each of which begins with a successive letter of the alphabet. But in chapter 3 each line in the 22 stanzas begins with a successive letter. Chapter 4 has 22 stanzas of 2 lines each, also in an acrostic pattern. The acrostic form is not found in chapter 5, but it is an "alphabetic" poem, insofar as it contains 22 lines. I mention these details to suggest that the poetic form may have been a contributing reason why the poems were kept together. But the fairly convincing reason is the first; they deal with the fall of Jerusalem in 587 even though chapter 3 is highly individualistic.

Q. 72. I can understand mourning over the deaths of human beings, but why should there be mourning over a city?

One might answer your question by replying that people were concerned in this destruction of Jerusalem—either killed or taken into captivity. But that really wouldn't answer your point. Jerusalem, or Zion, is the center of the Lamentations, at least in chapters 1, 2, and 4, where the city is personified. We touched briefly on the importance of the holy city in Q. 7 in discussing the "Songs of Zion," and in Q. 13 in the discussion of the royal psalms and messianism. But more needs to be said, because it is difficult for us to identify so fully with a city as ancient Israel did with Jerusalem.

One might think that the threats of the prophets, from Amos to Jeremiah, would have been enough to bring the people of God into line. But we need merely to read the description of the infidelities scored by these prophets to realize the failure of their words to strike home. It took such a shock as the destruction of Jerusalem to change them. As it is put in Jeremiah 31:31–34, there is to be a new covenant, unlike the one they broke, with the law now written in their hearts, and their sins forgiven. The poignant description of suffering in the book of Lamentations expresses the suffering that effected this change of heart.

What did the destruction of Jerusalem mean? Ezekiel graphically portrays the theological sense of it, when he describes the departure of the glory of the Lord in 11:23: "The glory of the Lord ascended from the middle of the city, and stopped on the mountain east of the city" (*NRSV*). The Lord was abandoning the holy place, where the divine residence on earth had been established. Israel was out of touch with the Almighty, and this was symbolized by the departure of the "glory" in the vision. This was an unheard of, an impossible, thing, for faithful

Israelites. One could think back to the many displays of divine forgiveness, and the powerful motives which Moses put before the Lord to secure the divine favor: "If only you would forgive their sin! If you will not, then strike me out of the book that you have written" (Deut 32:32). Moses could remind the Lord, "Remember your servants Abraham, Isaac and Israel... (32:13). The unconditional covenant with Abraham and the fathers—where was it? And so also the covenant with David, relative to his descendants on the throne in Jerusalem (2 Sam 7:15–16; Ps 89:34–38). Was the Lord going to abandon his people completely? The moving description of the personified Zion in the book of Lamentations is destined precisely to move the Lord to pity. Could the Lord who cried out in that marvelous soliloquy of Hosea 11:8–9, "How can I give you up...?" really have rejected the beloved? That was the paradox: God could and God did.

Q. 73. Why is the book of Lamentations so boring?

That's certainly a possibility. Perhaps you don't like acrostic poems (but in the acrostic style there is a built-in number that keeps a composition from being too long!). Or perhaps you don't utilize the poetic imagination that you are gifted with. Let us take some illustrations from the book. Thus, in chapter 1 there is a striking shift from a description of the suffering of Zion to a personification of the holy city itself:

> Come, all you who pass by the way,
>   look and see
> Whether there is any suffering like mine
>   which has been dealt me.... (1:12)
> At this I weep,
>   my eyes run with tears... (1:16)

This graphic effect is followed in chapter 2 by a fulsome description of the punishment: "The Lord has become an enemy" (2:5). The Lamentations reached musical and poetic heights in the days when they were used in the Tenebrae Office of Holy Week, with such lines as:

> To what can I liken or compare you,
> O daughter Jerusalem?
> What example can I show you for your comfort,
> virgin daughter Zion?
> For great as the sea is your downfall;
> who can heal you? (2:13)

In chapter 3 there is a sudden, unexpected change. The speaker is a single individual, identified:

> I am a man who knows affliction
> from the rod of his anger.... (3:1)

After twenty verses describing his desolation and suffering, the poet suddenly looks for hope, and finds it in recalling the traditional notions of the Lord's faithfulness and mercy. He seems to have undergone terrible, but unspecified, afflictions and he recognizes "it is good for a man to bear the yoke from his youth" (v 27). Affliction will be followed by the Lord's kindness and mercy. Finally, there is an admission of human sinfulness (v 39). The tone of lament is continued, and the individual speaker seems to be representative of the entire community that confidently invokes the Lord's aid and deliverance (vv 40–66).

The fourth poem returns to a description of Zion's woeful condition. Here the anointed or messiah (the reigning king) is called "our breath of life" (v 20), but the Davidic covenant is a thing of the past.

In the final chapter (22 lines, but not an acrostic) the community continues the lament, but in verse 19 there is a breakthrough—confidence in the Lord who is enthroned forever, and an impassioned plea for restoration.

There is much pathos, imagination and movement in these five poems. It remains for us to shed our own preconceptions and enter sympathetically into the situation of the remnant community.

Q. 74. Is there any history of the exiles in Babylon, 587–539?

There is a history of these exiles, but no one of them wrote it. The Lamentations reflect one aspect of this history: the sense of shock and compunction felt by the people. Within the Bible we can point to chapters 40–55 of the book of Isaiah, which reflect the spirited summons to faith in a future which an unknown prophet delivered to the exiles:

> Comfort, give comfort to my people,
>   says your God,
> Speak tenderly to Jerusalem, and proclaim to her
>   that her service is at an end,
>   her guilt is expiated;
> Indeed she has received from the hand of the Lord
>   double for all her sins (Is 40:1).

The words of this prophet are dated to about the middle of the sixth century, as Cyrus was making his bid to become the master of the area, conquering Babylon in 539. He then issued a decree permitting the Jews to return, and they did so in several waves, especially for the next twenty years, finally rebuilding the Temple in 515. But there were enclaves of Jewish residents throughout the area as for example, the community whom Ezekiel addressed at Tel-abib (Ezek 3:13). Others had gone down to Egypt (Jer 33–44).

There is little hard-nosed evidence concerning the fate of the Jewish people in the empire. The so-called Murashu tablets give evidence of some kind of "banking" activities, and include some Jewish names active in the fifth century. Some Jews may have prospered. Nehemiah is a trusted servant in the Persian court around 450 (Neh 1–2). It is generally presumed that during the Exile Israel must have gathered together and edited its traditions (e.g., a final edition of the Deuteronomistic history from Joshua to Kings). But we are woefully ignorant of this period.

1 AND 2 CHRONICLES AND EZRA-NEHEMIAH

Q. 75. Where can we find the history of Israel after its return to Jerusalem in 539?

The key books are those to be found among the Writings: Ezra-Nehemiah and 1–2 Chronicles. Ezra and Nehemiah were originally one work, Ezra, in the Jewish tradition. Early on (Origen, Jerome) they were separated, and this separation finally entered into the Hebrew Bible in the fifteenth century. However, the title of Nehemiah does not appear. It has often been assumed that this formed one historical work with 1–2 Chronicles (Ezra 1:1–3 is almost synonymous with 2 Chron 36:22–23). In the Writings they come before the books of Chronicles, which are the last books in the Hebrew Bible. Chronicles itself was originally one book but was divided into two at a later date. Chronicles (in Hebrew "the events of the days," or annals) was called *paraleipomena* in the Septuagint, meaning "things left over," or "left out," as though it were a supplement to 1–2 Kings. But this is quite misleading, as we shall see. Following the Septuagint and Vulgate tradition, most Bibles put Chronicles after Kings, followed by Ezra-Nehemiah. At the present time there is a dispute among scholars whether one author stands behind the four books (admittedly there are memoirs used in Ezra and Nehemiah). For convenience sake we will use the word Chronicler as a loose designation for the writer, with no pretence at a claim for authorship.

Q. 76. The names of these books are new to me; I have heard of 1 Esdras and 2 Esdras. Are they all the same?

The terminology for these books has become very complicated in the course of history. For the record, here is a table of equivalents:

1 Esdras: (This is also called Esdras A). A Greek translation of 2 Chronicles 35–36: Ezra 1–10, and Neh 8:1–13, plus the addition about the debate of Zerubbabel and the royal pages before King Darius about the strongest thing in the world (truth). In the Vulgate, this is called 3 Esdras, and is published in the appendix to the New Testament. The Vulgate uses the title 1 Esdras for what is now called Ezra.

2 & 3 Esdras: (Septuagint terminology) corresponds to the Hebrew Ezra and Nehemiah respectively.

4 Esdras: This is the Latin Vulgate terminology, but the book has come to be known as 2 Esdras, and is published among the apocrypha of the *NRSV*. We shall return to this important work in the questions concerning apocalypticism.

Q. 77. Would you also clarify for me the sequence of kingdoms and kings which are mentioned in the Writings?

Perhaps the best answer to your question is to refer you to the various lists of kings that appear in the *New Jerome Biblical Commentary*, at least to those on pages 407, 1233, 1242, 1245. But the highlights can be sketched here as a kind of guide to the questions and answers that appear in this booklet. Egypt appears throughout the Bible, more assertive at some times than others. In the eastern part of the Fertile Crescent, the important sequence of empires should be noted: Assyria (fall of Nineveh, 612), Babylon (or Neo-Babylonian empire; fall of Babylon, 539); Persia (from Cyrus, 550 to Darius III, 331). These empires are followed by Alexander the Great (d. 323), whose empire was divided up in four segments, two of which are very important for the Bible.

The Ptolemaic dynasty prevailed in Egypt, and during the third century the Jews in Palestine were subject to the various Ptolemies. During this time the Greek translation of the Bible was begun, as Greek tended to become the language of the Jews living in the Diaspora, or dispersion beyond Palestine.

The Seleucid dynasty was given Syria and established its capital at Antioch on the Orontes river. At the turn of the second century they made their move to take over Palestine, where they met with stiff resistance from the Jews (Maccabean wars). Finally, Simon Maccabeus achieves some measure of independence in 142 (1 Macc 13:41), and the Jews maintained their independence, despite difficulties, until the Romans took over in 63 B.C. incorporating Palestine into the Roman province of Syria.

It might be helpful to you to make up a card or two which would chart these and other important dates and kings/kingdoms, that you could keep as an insert in your Bible.

Q. 78. How many histories of Israel are there?

That is not an easy question to answer. As far as the Writings are concerned, the work of the Chronicler (including Ezra-Nehemiah) belongs to the "historical" genre. He had predecessors, and indeed it is clear that he relies on the books of Samuel and Kings particularly. You might well ask why the Chronicler wrote another history of Israel, when previous histories had already been written. What were these?

There is no perfect agreement on whether the following should be called "histories," but it will be helpful to review them if we are to understand the Chronicler.

A few words about the Pentateuch have to be said. During most of this century, at least four strands in the Pentateuch were accepted: JEPD. This general unanimity has been profoundly shaken. There had always been two uncertainties (among others): Was there ever an Elohist? Was the Priestly tradition a consecutive narrative? Despite the sea changes in the interpretation of the Pentateuch, it would be correct to say that the Yahwist or J source did constitute a history of sorts, being the most important narrative for the patriarchal and much of the Moses and desert happenings. Although its existence is controverted, the E or Elohist source modified the J traditions from the point of view of the northern kingdom. The portions attributed to P, or the Priestly source (e.g., the ten *toledot* or generations), can be singled out, but it is debatable if P was a continuous independent historical narrative, or is represented in the Pentateuch by a thoroughgoing revision of and additions to earlier sources. D is represented mainly by the book of Deuteronomy, and it is usually associated with the Deuteronomistic history.

The Deuteronomistic history (often abbreviated as Dtr) is in a sense the primary history of Israel, extending from Joshua through 2 Kings, roughly 1200 to 550. The reason for the name is the influence of deuteronomic theology on the individual(s) responsible for the work (e.g., the centrality of the Temple as the earthly residence of the Lord, etc.).

Among the Writings, the history we are concerned with is the work of the Chronicler: Ezra-Nehemiah and 1–2 Chronicles. Whether they were all the work of one person is disputed, but this question is less important in view of the clear fact that earlier and recognizable sources have entered into these books.

Q. 79. Why did the Chronicler write another history of the monarchical period, thus going over old familiar territory?

The answer lies in the particular theological interpretation which the Chronicler wished to offer to the people of his (post-exilic, perhaps fourth century) generation. He had his own ideas about the past and its significance for the present, and we shall attempt to give some brief examples.

He begins his history with genealogies, from Adam, no less, down to Saul (chaps. 1–9). The very idea of a string of genealogies at the opening of a history takes one aback. But even these genealogies betray the interests of the author: "All Israel," David and the royal dynasty, the importance of Judah and Jerusalem, the Levites, and the principle of retribution. Little concern is shown for Moses and the Exodus events. The covenants are left unmentioned; in a sense the real history begins with David. Emphasis is placed on the genealogies of Judah, David, and the Levites, for all this is leading up to the centrality of Jerusalem and the Temple.

One of the primary sources of the Chronicler is Samuel-Kings, and it is precisely in the differences from these books that we learn of his particular interests. He skips the details of David's rise to power and begins with Saul's death. He comes quickly to David's conquest of Jerusalem and arrangements for the future of the Temple and its liturgy (especially the Levites, 1 Chron 23–27). But the incident of David and Bathsheba is not mentioned. An interesting interpretation of 2 Samuel 24:1 is given. Instead of "The Lord's anger against Israel flared again, and he incited David against the Israelites by prompting him to number Israel and Judah," we read in 1 Chronicles 21:1: "A Satan rose up against Israel, and he enticed David into taking a census of Israel." There can hardly be a more dramatic change than from the Lord to Satan. Here one catches a glimpse into the evolving figure of a malevolent Satan, which will come to a head in the activities of the devil in the New Testament. The census-taking was apparently looked upon as insulting to the Lord, a failure to rely upon God for the needs of the nation. As usual, God is the one who punishes the wrongdoing and the calamity can be ended only by appeasing God (2 Sam 24:15–17; 1 Chron 21:7–15).

The Temple and its worship is, of course, the center of the Chronicler's interest, and 2 Chronicles 1–9 is given over to its construction and Solomon's role. The breakup of the monarchy into Israel and Judah is a good example of the Chronicler's agenda. Since he is interpreting the history of the Jews living in and around Jerusalem, he restricts his "history" to what happened to the kingdom of Judah. He does not treat the kingdom of Israel in and for itself. But he is also generous to the north in that he never mentions the "sin of Jeroboam" (worship at the sanctuaries of Dan and Bethel). Indeed, the northern kingdom fares well when it is portrayed as open to the Passover celebration of King Hezekiah of Judah (2 Chron 30:1–22). The role of the priests and the Levites in all the liturgical undertakings is highlighted.

Q. 80. What is meant by the "restoration" at the end of the Exile?

From the point of view of time, it designates the events extending from 539 to at least 515 when the Temple in Jerusalem was rebuilt. From the point of view of important historical figures, those involved are Cyrus, and the leaders of the returning exiles: Sheshbazzar (Ezra 1:8); Jeshua and Zerubbabel (Ezra 2:2; 3:2,8; 5:2) who receive encouragement from the prophets Haggai and Zechariah (Ezra 5:2; 6:14). As mentioned before, the exiles returned in several waves (even as late as Ezra himself, perhaps 458). Ezra 2 (=Nehemiah 7) gives the names of various officials, priests, Levites and others; it is clear that the restored Judah (or *Yehud*, as it came to be called) was relatively small and grouped around Jerusalem as the key settlement. Serious and lasting opposition arose between the returnees and the people already dwelling in Palestine. The returnees tended to be exclusive, and to prevent the occupants from sharing in the rebuilding of the Temple (Ezra 4:1-4). The schism between the Jews and the Samaritans was a gradual process that came to a head a few centuries later.

Not much is known about Sheshbazzar (Ezra 1:8, "a prince of Judah"), who is said to have brought back the precious vessels of the Temple destroyed by Nebuchadnezzar in 587. The real action begins in 520 when the prophets galvanize Jeshua the high priest and Zerubbabel (in Haggai, called "governor") into rebuilding the Temple. From Haggai and Zechariah it has been inferred that more than Temple worship was involved. Messianic hopes were stirred, centered on the reestablishment of the Davidic dynasty under Zerubbabel who seems to have been a descendant of King Jehoiachin who died in exile at Babylon (1 Kgs 24:1–34). The details of this messianic movement are not clear, but it seems to have made an impression (Hag 2:20–23; Zech 4:1–14; 6:9–15). But Zerubbabel suddenly disappears from the scene. Nothing is said in any historical sources to explain his disappearance. Perhaps, as some scholars infer, Persia would not tolerate the resurgence of Davidic messianism, and simply put an end to the movement by removing Zerubbabel. In any case, it is the high priest and the high priestly line that becomes the de facto head of the community, even though all remain part (a mere fraction) of the Persian empire. The Temple was finally rebuilt and dedicated in 515 (Ezra 6:14–22). The obstacles from within and without the community were overcome (cf. Ezra 4–6).

Now you have the bare bones of the restoration, and you can see how bare it is. The picture is tantalizing, because more is suggested than is said. Uncertainty prevails over the entire history of the community during the Persian period. Even the detailed activity of Ezra and of Nehemiah cover only a short span in the fifth century. It is well-nigh impossible to put together a history of Judah in the post-exilic period until the Maccabean period (Antiochus Epiphanes began to reign about 175).

Q. 81. You have been quoting from the book of Ezra. How important a character is he?

Ezra is like a new Moses in Jewish tradition, a very important person, despite the fact that Sirach 49:13 passes over him in silence, while praising Nehemiah. We will first describe him on the basis of the book named after him. Immediately we run into a problem with his dating. According to Ezra 7:7–8, he led a group of people and officials to Jerusalem in the seventh year of Artaxerxes. This would be 458, for Artaxerxes I. Some have argued for Artaxerxes II, about fifty years later, in 398. There are difficulties in any solution, but let us accept 458, almost a century after the edict of Cyrus.

What was his office? Artaxerxes describes him as a priest, "the scribe of the law of the God of heaven" (Ezra 7:12; cf. also 7:6). The extent of his authority as "scribe" is not indicated, but in Nehemiah 8:1–3 Ezra reads out the law (presumably the Pentateuch or some form of it) to the people. Moreover, even high officials and priests and Levites come to him to study the law (Neh 8:13).

This description of Ezra fails to mention the lively way in which he communicates himself and his interests. There is great nobility expressed in his preparing for the trip. He blesses the Lord, the God of the fathers, who moved the king to glorify the Temple and turned the king's favor to him. His preparation for the trip is described thus: "Then I proclaimed a fast...that we might humble ourselves before our God to petition from him a safe journey for ourselves, our children, and all our possessions. For I would have been ashamed to ask the king for troops and horsemen to protect us against enemies along the way, since we had said to the king, 'The favoring hand of our God is upon all who seek him, but his mighty wrath is against all who forsake him.' So we fasted and prayed to our God for this, and our petition was granted" (Ezra 8:21–23).

His religious work is manifested in his authority and ability to explain the law, and one can only applaud him in this. What is less attractive to the modern reader is the reform concerning mixed marriages which he pushes through. One need not doubt the sincerity of the man himself—his prayer in 9:3–15 (see also Neh 9:6–37) is a spectacular and moving event. But the decision to separate the Jews from foreign women they had married is drastic. This dismissal of foreign women and the children they had begotten is very hard to countenance. It has been said that Jewish exclusivism was necessary at this time. The people recognized the Exile as a punishment for following the ways of Canaanites and foreigners. But there could have been other means to anticipate similar temptations in the future than to expel foreigners.

Q. 82. Was Nehemiah as important as Ezra?

Yes, he is, although in Jewish tradition Ezra has outrun him in acquiring greater fame, and being the "author" of many works (See Q. 76). The book named after him begins in the first person (two sections are conveniently called the "Nehemiah Memoirs"; 1:1–7:5; 11:1–13:31). He describes himself as a cupbearer—an important position, with the responsibility of making sure that the royal table is not served poison—to Artaxerxes I, and the year is about 445. He is upset by the news that Jerusalem's walls have been breeched (apparently recently). His intimate terms with the king are clear from the way his sadness betrays itself, and from the king's inquiry. His request to go to Jerusalem is readily granted and he is off to the holy city. Early on, his opponents are mentioned, Sanballat the Horonite, apparently the governor of Samaria, and Tobiah from Ammon to the east. He conducts a circumspect tour of the city walls by night, and organizes a task force to rebuild the wall. Continuous opposition comes from his enemies, first in terms of ridicule, and then in threats to battle with Nehemiah. The vivid description follows: "From that time on, only half my able men took a hand in the work, while the other half, armed with spears, bucklers...stood guard behind the whole house of Judah. The load carriers, too, were armed; each did his work with one hand, and held a weapon with the other" (4:10–11). In addition to these physical dangers, the economic situation was bad. Usury and oppression afflicted the little people, and Nehemiah rises to the occasion to institute a reform (Neh 5:1–13). It is almost by chance that he refers to his twelve-year governance in Jerusalem. The opposition from Sanballat and others continues, and Nehemiah is threatened with personal harm.

Finally the wall is finished ("in fifty-two days," Neh 6:15), and the dedication is celebrated with great pomp (12:27–43). But the work of Nehemiah is not over. When he returns after twelve years to Jerusalem, he introduces various reforms. The Levites had been neglected, and now tithes were enforced, and the sabbath observed. The problem of mixed marriages had to be faced again. The book ends with one of Nehemiah's frequent requests for himself: "Remember this in my favor, O my God!" (13:31; cf. 5:19; 6:14; 13:14).

I have presented a brief summary of the highlights, so as to give a sense of the person of Nehemiah. The problems concerning the dating, and his relationship to Ezra have to be passed over.

Q. 83. How can I put together the post-exilic period as a whole?

You are not the only one who has this difficulty; I suggested something of this at the end of Q. 80. The historical details are uncertain, and in many cases they are not very illuminating. Let me try another approach—just how important is this post-exilic period? It is much more than the mere fact that the Temple is rebuilt or the city walls established. It was a creative period culturally, in that the traditions which had been in the process of being handed down, reevaluated and rewritten, were now being assembled in something close to the final form of the Tanak (recall that in the second century B.C. there is a sense of the law and the prophets as two bodies of material, and there is a nebulous third, "other books"; see Q. 1). Most of the precious wisdom literature is post-exilic in its written form (Job is hard to date).

Between Nehemiah (445) and the Maccabean revolt (168–65), the Jewish community passed from one domination to another: Persian, Greek with the Hellenistic division of the Ptolemies in Egypt (third century), and the Seleucids in Antioch (from 200 on). The political and social conditions of this time are not well known since our sources are so sparse (see M. Hengel, *Judaism and Hellenism* [Philadelphia: Fortress, 1974] 2 vols.).

DANIEL AND APOCALYPTIC

Q. 84. Why are you treating Daniel at the end? It doesn't come at the end in the list of the Writings, does it?

You are right; it is the ninth in the list of the Writings. We must also recall that the sequence of the books within the Writings varies in the Jewish tradition; besides, the relative position is of practically no consequence, provided all the books are treated.

The real reason is the historical sequence. Our questions have tended to follow an historical sequence with the treatment of 1–2 Chronicles and Ezra-Nehemiah. But the history in these works just barely introduces us to the post-exilic period. As we shall see, the book of Daniel is pertinent to several centuries in this period, especially to the Maccabean era (second century).

Another reason is the apocalyptic nature of several chapters in the book of Daniel. This work is the first pure apocalypse in the Old Testament. Thus it provides a fitting opportunity to discuss this kind of literature that seems so strange to us. Moreover, it forms a bridge into the New Testament, where the book of "Revelation" (for that is what apocalypse means) occurs.

Q. 85. I am confused by such terms as apocalyptic, apocalypticism, and eschatology. Can you define them for me?

It is impossible to give a strict definition of these terms. Scholars themselves differ in the way in which they understand these concepts. But a broad descriptive definition can be provided as a preliminary guide.

First, it has been noted that the basic term occurs in the New Testament to designate the last book, the Apocalypse (or Revelation) of John. As Revelation 1:1 puts it, "The revelation of Jesus Christ, which God gave to him, to show his servants what must happen soon. He made it known by sending his angel to his servant John." Certain basic elements of an apocalypse appear in this verse. It speaks of a revelation from God—a revelation that bears on the future (what is to happen soon). The seer is God's "servant John" to whom the angel will give the revelation. This verse is not intended to be a definition, and it can be expanded, as we shall see, by comparison with other apocalypses that have been written in the centuries just prior to and after the Christian era.

"Apocalyptic" is an adjective, (often used as a noun), and should designate the literature that contains the traits and phenomena of apocalypse. Because there are so many different apocalypses which have been written it is used loosely to designate all of them, such as *1 Enoch*. Apocalypticism is a noun which designates the movements which gave birth to this literature and the characteristic worldview that is associated with it.

For our purposes the definition of J. J. Collins in the *NJBC* (19:4; p. 299) will serve as a handy reference: "An apocalypse is defined by both form and content: as a genre of revelatory literature, mediated by an angel or heavenly being, which is concerned with a transcendent world populated by angels and with transcendent eschatology which has a personal as well as a cosmic dimension." On this basis, *1 Enoch* (one of the so-called pseudepigrapha) and Daniel are the earliest apocalypses in the Hellenistic period. Other portions of the Old Testament are classified as apocalyptic (e.g., the so-called "little apocalypse" of Isaiah 24–27) but this is a loose usage. The description suits admirably the book of Daniel. In chapters 7, 8, 9, and 10–12 Daniel has a series of visions which are explained to him by heavenly visitors (e.g., Gabriel, in 8:16). When we analyze these visions we will see that divine decisions are taken in a "transcendent world"—they have to do with what will happen personally and cosmically. Finally, the hero of the apocalypse is usually a figure from hoary antiquity (e.g., Enoch).

Eschatology derives from the Greek word, *eschatos*, meaning "last" and this is applied to time and things: the end time, the last things. It is characterized by a definitive intervention of God in history, whether for weal or for woe. Many ideas have clustered around it, such as messianism and covenant. It plays a large role in the apocalyptic literature, since the visions often bear on the end time.

Q. 86. These definitions are too abstract for me. Can you give me some concrete examples?

Your reaction is well taken. The only way to get into this type of literature is to read the works that are so classified. We will concentrate on Daniel, but we can begin by describing briefly one of the outstanding apocalyptic writings, *1 Enoch*. Although it is not in the Bible, it is filled with biblical allusions and, of course, the hero is Enoch of Genesis 5:21–24, who "walked with God...and then God took him." Actually this book is a collection of several different writings dating probably from the fourth century to the turn of the Christian era (see the English translation in J. Charlesworth, ed. *Old Testament Pseudepigrapha* [Doubleday: Garden City, N.Y., 1983–87] 2 vols.). We will attempt to communicate a feel for apocalypticism by sampling some of the collections.

The "book of the Watchers" is interesting because it expands the well known but mysterious passage of Genesis 6:1–4, in which the sons of God unite with the daughters of men, and the Nephilim, or giants, are begotten. These sons of God are the Watchers, who have spread evil, and are eventually condemned by God. What is going on behind the Enoch story? Some think there is reference to the successors of Alexander (also called Diadochoi), who took over the Fertile Crescent and hellenized it. In any case it must refer to some crisis which has been veiled by the author by utilizing the myth of Enoch and the episode in Genesis 6. But there is another plane of reality that is intended: the supernatural, or the events that transpire in the heavenly court. Enoch becomes the mediator of this supernatural revelation. He sees the throne of God and journeys with angels all over creation. Especially revealing are the weapons and places of judgment where the spirits of the dead will end up: punishment for the sinners, reward for the righteous, and then another place for those who have already been punished for their sins. The problem of retribution, long a conundrum to the Israelites (see QQ. 29–30, 61) is situated in the cosmos, not merely in the life of an individual, such as Job. This "other" world has been travelled by Enoch, and judgment of the wicked is now assured. It is after death that their judgment takes place. This kind of imaginative writing is designed for moments of crisis; one must not give up—the righteous will be preserved and the wicked punished. The point is that the decisions from on high affect the events of this world, and we shall see that principle at work in the book of Daniel.

Q. 87. Did Daniel really exist?

This question is like the one asked about Job 9 (see Q. 25). The shortest answer would be another question: which Daniel? We might as well begin there, for there is more than one Daniel in the book named after him. We remember from Q. 25 that Job was bracketed with figures of antiquity: Noah and Danel (of Ugaritic legend). Jewish tradition identified this Danel with the Daniel known from the later portion of the Writings (in other words, the Daniel who appears in the book named after him). But the "Daniel" of Ezekiel 14:14,20 (and cf. 28:3) seems to have existed only in imaginative tradition, not in reality.

Then who is the Daniel who is the hero of the book named after him? All we know about him is from that book, and he appears to have at least two personalities. Daniel I is the figure in chapters 1–6, and also in the deuterocanonical additions to the book, the story of Bel and the Dragon, and of Susanna (chaps. 13–14). Daniel II is the visionary of chapters 7, 8, 9 and 10–12. This is the truly apocalyptic figure who has visions and to whom mysteries are revealed by the means of an angel.

Is there any connection between Daniel I and II? I would suggest this possible explanation. The Maccabean author, who writes about

165 B.C. concerning the visionary Daniel—this is where the main interest lies and apocalypticism appears—chose the name Daniel because it was well known from the stories (chaps. 1–6, in which Daniel I figures) that had circulated in the previous centuries. He placed this Daniel back in the exilic period (Nebuchadnezzar and Belshazzar are from this time). In Daniel 9:1–2 this Daniel is portrayed as meditating on the word of the Lord to Jeremiah concerning the seventy years before the exile would end (cf. Jer 24:11–12; 29:10).

So the answer to your question is complicated, due to the composition of the book itself. This explanation will doubtless call forth other questions about the book.

Q. 88. Explain more about how the literary structure of the book of Daniel helps us to know when it was written.

If you read the first six chapters carefully, you will note that they are all in the third person, speaking *about* Daniel, and describing the adventures of him and his companions. This is in marked contrast to the following chapters (7–12), in which Daniel speaks in the first person about visions and revelations explained to him by an angel. There is a different texture, so to speak, to each section: wonders on the one hand, and the revelation of mysteries on the other.

However, there is a complication: two languages are used—Hebrew in 1:1–2:4a and in chapters 8–12, but Aramaic in 2:4b–7:28. So there is an overlap here. In addition, there is a concentric structure to chapters 2–7: 2 and 7 deal with kingdoms; 3 and 6 describe wonderful deliverances; 4 and 5 present divine judgments on kings. Although the alternation of the languages, Hebrew and Aramaic, remains without adequate explanation, there is still no reason to deny the two halves of the book.

More can be said about chapters 1–6. Each of these chapters illustrates some practical theological point. Chapter 1 describes how fidelity to the biblical laws concerning food enables Daniel and his companions to excel above anyone else, both in health and in wisdom, in Nebuchadnezzar's court. Chapter 2 indicates that Daniel's wisdom given him by God, is superior to all else, since he interprets Nebuchadnezzar's dream (the contents of the dream are similar to the visions of chapters 7–9). In chapter 3 Daniel's companions refuse to worship the golden statue of King Nebuchadnezzar, and are delivered by their God from the fiery furnace (note their complete submission to God in 3:16–18). Chapter 4 illustrates Daniel's wisdom once again as he interprets a dream referring to Nebuchadnezzar's madness. In chapter 5 Daniel interprets the handwriting on the wall for King Belshazzar (cf. chap. 2). Finally, Daniel is delivered from the lion's den, because of fidelity to his God (chap. 6).

When is it likely that such stories would have arisen? Many have claimed that what we have here is an underground literature that circulated during the persecution of the Jews in the Maccabean period. They *can* fit into such a context, but not necessarily. The Maccabean context would naturally call for hostile royalty, a king (Antiochus Epiphanes, it would be understood) who persecutes the people of God. But in chapters 1–6 the kings are in fact weak and ineffectual, but not hostile. It is true that the stories point up the blessings of fidelity to the law, but these lessons would be appropriate at any time, and also during the post-exilic period when the Persians and later the Greeks ruled.

In addition, chapter 4 has received a remarkable illustration from one of the Dead Sea scrolls, the fragment known as the "Prayer of Nabonidus." Nabonidus was the last king of Babylon, and for a long time it was known that he had been away from the capital for several years down in Tema, an oasis in northern Arabia. The fragment, written in the first person by this king, tells of his sojourn in Tema for seven years because of a sickness. Then a Jewish seer explains to the king why this has happened. Even though the text from Qumran is fragmentary, there can hardly be any doubt that there must be some connection between the story it contains and the madness of Nebuchadnezzar (not Nabonidus, it is true) in chapter 4.

It is reasonable, therefore, to consider the opening chapters of Daniel as adventures at court, stories about the deliverance the Lord provides for faithful servants. They would have circulated during the fourth and third centuries, and were seen in the Maccabean period as tales which could strengthen the faith of the persecuted Jews. Hence in their *present* context—the context of a book that has the Maccabean period principally in mind—they are applicable to the situation of the second century and the days of Antiochus Epiphanes.

Q. 89. Why do you say that the context of the book is the Maccabean struggle with Antiochus Epiphanes?

Briefly, the reason lies in the historical perspective given by the explanation of the visions of Daniel in chapters 7–12. Antiochus Epiphanes is not mentioned by name. Remember that Daniel is seeing the events to come in visions granted him in the sixth century. But there are several allusions that fit the persecution of Antiochus Epiphanes. The "changing of the times and the law" (Dan 7:25) refers to the suppression of feasts (2 Macc 6:6) and also to the persecution of those who observed the Torah (1 Macc 1:41–64). Perhaps the strongest reason is that throughout the visions of animals and the sequence of kingdoms in chapters 7–8, a Hellenistic king and his reign are singled out in a period of great stress for the people of God. This is Antiochus Epiphanes. The Jews will prevail, but there is no escape from the persecution from which they will be eventually delivered. More details about Antiochus Epiphanes—again without mentioning the name—are presented in Daniel 11:31–39. Those details are very, very specific, so much so that they appear to be prophecy after the fact (*vaticinium ex eventu*). The writer knows at first hand the persecution of 168–165, and he alludes to this situation. For the most part the apocalyptic style is less specific. The language is symbolic, and needs a heavenly mediator to explain it.

You may wonder why there is such an indirect style of describing the historical situation. That is the style favored by apocalyptic writings. But we must acknowledge the power of the symbolism, despite the indefiniteness of the details. These symbols become, as it were, eternal, representing the power of evil in any age—and also the power of God in overcoming evil. The visions are not limited merely to a specific historical period. They have implications for the broader history of humankind. They come to be used with ever new meanings, for example, in the book of Revelation in the New Testament. It is characteristic of the apocalyptic worldview that no one situation really exhausts the meaning of the symbol, and the symbols have lived on.

Q. 90. What is the "abomination of desolation"?

This is a symbol that has lived on. It is a traditional English translation of a phrase used to designate the altar to Zeus Olympus erected by

Antiochus Epiphanes in the Temple about 168 B.C. The original phrase can be also translated as the "abomination that makes desolate" (*NAB*, *NRSV*) or "appalling desolation" (*NJV*). (See Dan 11:31; 12:11; 1 Macc 1:54.) It is also found on the lips of Jesus in the New Testament. In Mark 13:14 it refers to the Roman power that profaned the Temple in A.D. 70, and perhaps even to an event before the return of the Son of man.

The abomination is mentioned in connection with times: "a time, two times, and a half a time" (Dan 9:27); probably this refers to three and a half years, roughly the duration of the persecution of the Jews (168–65). But there are several other mysterious references to times in the book: 2300 evenings and mornings (8:14) and 1290 days (12:11). The precise symbolism of these numbers escapes us.

Q. 91. Where can I find the prayer of the Three Young Men?

It is not in the Hebrew Bible, but it is found in the Greek Bible, or Septuagint. In the *NRSV* it appears as an insertion between Daniel 3:23 and 3:24, among the Apocrypha. In the *NAB* it appears at Daniel 3:52–90.

One should distinguish between the prayer of Azariah (*NAB* Dan 3:25–45) and the prayer of the three young men (*NAB* Dan 3:52–90). Azariah's prayer is in fact a communal confession (e.g., *NAB* 3:29, "we have sinned and transgressed by departing from you, and we have done every kind of evil"), resembling the prayer of Daniel 9:4–19. God is justified in the punishment that has been inflicted on a sinful people. Hence, there is a plea that God not abandon them, but rather remember the covenant with Abraham, and let their contrite spirit replace the Temple sacrifices that are absent. Let the Lord deliver them and let all "know that you alone are the Lord God, glorious over the whole world" (v 45). It is not easy to explain why this communal confession is on the lips of Azariah. It really cannot be applied to Azariah or his companions, for the three young men have demonstrated their fidelity to God by refusing to worship the statue set up by Nebuchadnezzar. Indeed, their profession of faith is admirable: "If our God, whom we serve can save us from the white-hot furnace and from your hands, O king, may he save us! But even if he will not, know, O king, that we will not serve your god or worship the golden statue which you set up" (3:17–18). The spirit of the prayer, however, is one of humble admission of sin and justification of punishment—in other words, the theology that is characteristic of Deuteronomy.

The prayer of Azariah is separated from the prayer of the three young men by a paragraph (vv 46–51), describing how the angel of the Lord protected them, and thus it introduces the prayer in verse 51, "these three in the furnace with one voice sang, glorifying and blessing God" (v 51). What follows is a hymn in praise of God. The prayer calls upon all creatures, all the elements, and even Hananiah, Azariah and Mishael, to bless the Lord who delivered them from the fire. The hymn is reminiscent of several psalms, such as 136 and 148. In the case of the three youths, fire had lost its normal qualities (although it didn't fail to afflict Nebuchadnezzar's servants (3:22,48). It is clear that this is not a story that is aimed against Antiochus Epiphanes, because at the end of the story, Nebuchadnezzar acknowledges the God of Israel (3:95 *NAB*; 3:28 *NRSV*). There is no indication of any conversion of a monarch like Antiochus in chapters 7–12. Rather, it is a story that exalts the power of the Lord, who delivers those who are faithful to him. Such a message was pertinent at any time, and of course also during the time of the Maccabean troubles.

Q. 92. What is the meaning of the handwriting on the wall?

Your question refers to the fabulous feast of King Belshazzar (a son of Nabonidus, and despite Daniel 5:11, never really a king—but he acted as regent in the absence of Nabonidus). His blasphemous action consists in using the sacred Temple vessels while honoring "the gods of gold and silver, bronze and iron, wood and stone" (Dan 5:4). The mysterious handwriting on the wall is described by the effect that it has on the king. As in chapter 2, only Daniel is wiser than the wisest in Babylon, and he proceeded to interpret the mysterious *mene, teqel, peres* (following a slight change in the Masoretic text, showing three, not four words). Daniel's interpretation is quite clearly aimed at the end of Belshazzar and his kingdom. His days have been (1) "numbered" (ended); (2) he has been weighed and counts for naught; (3) his kingdom is to be divided between the Medes and the Persians. This punning explanation fits the context but the question can also be asked if these three Aramaic words have other meanings. The fact is that they designate three monetary weights: the mina, the shekel, and the half mina. Various theories have referred these terms to kings who succeeded Nebuchadnezzar, but these views have carried little weight.

The reaction of Belshazzar is what one might expect in a folk tale. Daniel is given royal privileges, even though he has just announced the end of Belshazzar's reign! We know nothing about the latter's end (5:30). Actually we know that Babylon yielded and was taken over peacefully by the army of Cyrus, but in 5:30 (*NAB* and MT, 6:1) we meet the mysterious Darius the Mede who follows the Babylonian (or Chaldean) monarch.

I say that this character is mysterious since his presence—even his existence—cannot be readily explained. He cannot be identified with Darius the Great, the successor to Cyrus who allowed the Jews to return in 539–38. We know of no king Darius who was from Media. There existed in the ancient world the idea of a succession of four world empires: Assyria (replaced in the Old Testament by Babylon), Media and Persia—followed, of course, by Greece. This sequence is followed in the portrayal of kingdoms in the visions of Daniel, but the fact is that the Medes were conquered by the Persians (Cyrus) before the latter took over world hegemony from the Babylonians. The most conspicuous role of Darius the Mede is in chapter 6, the story of Daniel in the lions' den. He is practically forced against his will to throw Daniel to the lions (cf. 6:17, 21, 24–27). The story has a variant in the deuterocanonical/apocryphal additions, Daniel 14:28–42.

Q. 93. What is the connection between Daniel and Jeremiah?

The connection between them is seen in chapter 9. Daniel is preoccupied with the passages in Jeremiah (25:11–12; 29:10) where the prophet speaks of "seventy years" as the length of time that Israel would be desolate. He doesn't seem to have any problem with the exact number of years, and seventy itself is a symbolic number. The situation is now toward the end of the Babylonian exile, and Daniel is pondering the meaning of the seventy years—which is explained to him by Gabriel as seventy weeks of years (490). His prayer is a confession of sin offered for the people (v 5, "we have sinned and done wrong..."). It is marked by anthological style—i.e., it is a mosaic of phrases that occur elsewhere in the Bible (the resemblance to Baruch 1:15–2:19 is particularly remarkable).

This device of 490 years enables the author to come quickly to his point, the last seven years. The first week of years extends from the beginning of the exile to its end. At that time appears the "anointed leader" (v 25), who is probably Jeshua the high priest. The middle years of this vision (62 weeks of years, i.e., 434), is simply passed over in order to reach the Maccabean period when "an anointed one" will be cut down. This refers to the beginning of the last week of years, when the anointed high priest, Onias III, is slain (171 B.C.; cf. 2 Macc 4:1–38). We are in the disastrous period of Antiochus Epiphanes and his campaign against the Temple and the Jews. Nonetheless, Antiochus secures agreement from "many" Jews (v 27). In this final "week," for half that time (168–165), he put an end to sacrifice and put up the abomination of desolation (see Q. 90). What is to take place after that is not indicated; for this we must go to the vision of chapter 7.

Q. 94. I thought that the "anointed one" in 9:26 is the messiah, and this would be Jesus Christ. What is the problem with saying this?

It is true that "anointed" and "messiah" may have reference to the same physical action: anointing (of king, or of high priest), but the word "anointed" is not an automatic reference to the promised messiah (or, as Christians would believe, to the Christ of the New Testament). The Lord views Cyrus as "anointed," an honor given to him because he had been chosen to fulfill a specific purpose (ultimately to free Israel from the Babylonian exile; Is 45:1). Hence, we must try to understand what is meant by "anointed" in its specific context. It is true that a venerable tradition took the "anointed" of Daniel 9:26 to refer to Christ. Besides the violence inflicted upon this anointed, there was another reason: the perspective of the Roman empire—in other words, the time frame of that interpretation is different from the one we are working with. The sequence of kings/kingdoms, in our view, ends with the Seleucid ruler, Antiochus Epiphanes, and not with the Romans. In this view, there is no possibility of a reference beyond the Maccabean period to the death of Christ. To repeat, the anointed of Daniel 9:26 is Onias III, murdered in 171 B.C.

Q. 95. Who is the "son of man" in the book of Daniel?

Your question refers to the famous vision of the four beasts in the seventh chapter of Daniel. Daniel sees four different beasts coming up out of the sea, all of them "like" some animal, a lion, a bear and leopard (cf. Hos 13:7–8). These three beasts correspond to the three kingdoms in the vision of the statue of four metals seen by Daniel in chapter 2: the sequence of the Babylonians, Medes and Persians. As always there is a particular kingdom the author is interested in—the final one, or Greek empire (feet of iron and clay in chapter 2; the ten-horned beast of chapter 7). The three beasts are the kings/kingdoms we have seen before: Babylon, Medes and Persians. They yield to the terrible fourth beast (the Greek empire), and the attention is focused on the "little horn" of this final beast. It has human eyes, and an arrogant speech: Antiochus Epiphanes. This terrifying vision of the beasts of chaos turns into a judgment scene as the "Ancient of days" appears, and the "son of man" is presented before him. Judgment is passed on all the beasts, and the son of man receives "dominion, glory, and kingship." But Daniel presses on and wants to know more about the formidable and horned fourth beast. The little horn (obviously Antiochus Epiphanes) arising from this beast will make war against "the holy ones" but ultimately the holy ones prevail, thanks to the intervention of the Ancient One, the Most High. Ultimately, kingship and dominion is given to the "holy people of the Most High" (7:27).

The symbolism of this passage creates some difficulties for us. It is clear that the Jewish people are those who triumph, but how can they be identified with the "son of man" and also with the "holy ones" (7:14, 27)? Although "holy ones" usually designates the angels, this is not always so (e.g., Ps 34:10). Therefore, one can take the son of man as a symbol of the people of God who triumph over Antiochus Epiphanes. The dominion and kingship given to the son of man (7:14) is given to the holy ones (7:18, 22), i.e., to the Jews. It is not strange that the community be symbolized in an individual. One can point elsewhere in the Old Testament to the fluctuation between the individual and the community: several "I" psalms (e.g., Ps 44:5–7), or the Servant songs in Isaiah (e.g., chap. 53).

Hence the short answer to your question is that the "son of man" in Daniel represents the faithful Jewish community. But one can hardly raise this question apart from the New Testament usage of the phrase applied to Jesus. The phrase itself merely means a mortal man; in Hebrew it occurs over a hundred times, mainly in the book of Ezekiel, referring to the prophet. In Daniel there is the comparative usage, "like," hence, "one like a human being." This seems to be a symbol, just as the beasts from the sea are symbols. The New Testament usage is practically restricted to the gospels. Here "son of man" is a title applied to Jesus, both by himself and by others. But it remains a mysterious title. It is used in so many contexts: Jesus' earthly ministry; his death and resurrection, and as an eschatological or future figure. As an example of the puzzle which it presents, one may read Matthew 11:18–19, where the title is used in connection with the accusation of Jesus being a glutton and drunkard. I bring up this New Testament usage, not to give an answer to it, but merely to say that it does not have the same connotation as the phrase in Daniel 9. It has to be examined on its own merits, in the gospels themselves.

Q. 96. Is there a doctrine of the resurrection in the book of Daniel?

Yes, corporal resurrection is definitely referred to in 12:2–3: "Many of those who sleep in the dust of the earth shall awake, some to everlasting life, and some to shame and everlasting contempt. Those who are wise shall shine like the brightness of the sky, and those who lead many to righteousness, like the stars forever and ever."

For the first time in the Bible there is indisputable reference to a glorious life after death. Not even Isaiah 26:19, "Your dead shall live, your corpses (Heb: my corpse) shall rise," is unquestionable. The vision of the resurrection (or resuscitation) of the bones in Ezekiel 37 refers to the revival of Israel as a people. It may very well be that the period of the martyrs, the Maccabean period, contributed to the flowering of this belief (cf. 2 Macc 7:23). Daniel is not speaking of a universal resurrection; the faithful will arise to "everlasting life"—they are the concern of the writer because their names are found "written in the book" (12:1). Some think that the wicked are not included in resurrection (12:2), but they probably are, just as in the Wisdom of Solomon the good and the evil are distinguished in the life beyond death (Wis 1:15–16; 2:24–3:1). However, in the book of Wisdom the *manner* or mode of entering the next life is not specified—neither resurrection nor the immortal nature of the soul.

Special mention is made of "those who are wise" (the *maskilim*); they will "shine like the stars forever and ever" (12:3). Their suffering and eventual victory "at the time of the end" was noted in 11:33–35. Although no such resurrection of the just took place, the hope was merely postponed, never abandoned. This doctrine of the resurrection entered the Christian era with divided support. The Sadducees denied it (Acts 23:8) in contradistinction to the Pharisees who affirmed it. The doctrine formed the background for the resurrection of Christ (1 Cor 15:16, "if there is no resurrection of the dead, then Christ has not been raised").

Q. 97. I am not comfortable with the book of Daniel. It is not what it claims to be, a work written by a man named Daniel. Was this a common literary practice?

Perhaps your discomfort comes from the fact that the work is an apocalypse, and these writings are anything but clear. Perhaps also you have been accustomed to regard it as a prophecy, since it is placed in English Bibles after Ezekiel. At the heart of your question, however, is the problem of pseudonymity, i.e., a second century writer writes in the name of someone who is situated back in the sixth century. That is a problem for our culture, but it was not a problem in the ancient world where authorship was interpreted in a manner different from our conception. Thus, Ecclesiastes is given out in the superscription (Eccl 1:1) as the son of David, presumably Solomon, as Jewish and Christian tradition understood it. The Pentateuch or Torah could be attributed to Moses, even though most of it was written after his time. When we come to apocalyptic we must learn to accept a different point of view on "authorship." Those who have the heavenly revelations are usually heroes of old: Enoch, Ezra, Abraham, Daniel. This was simply the practice in the Hellenistic age. They did not recognize our "problem," and tell us why they chose such figures. One may reason that this practice was to give authority to the works. It should be noted that the truly important persons are the heavenly figures, angels that mediate the revelation to the various characters. The practice of pseudonymity, then, is not with the intention to deceive. Apocalypticism simply doesn't think that way. It delivers its message in its own style and on its own terms.

Perhaps this reply may strike you as too slick: what appears to be a deception is not a deception. Yet, in reply, one can point to all the various pseudonymous writings in the intertestamental period especially. Another reply would be to go through the book of Daniel, item by item, a kind of a posteriori proof, in order to see that this apocalypse could have been written only in connection with the Maccabean period.

CONCLUSION

Q. 98. Can one speak of a "theology" of the Writings, as one might speak of a "theology" of the Pentateuch or of the prophets?

I was once asked to write an article on that very topic, the theology of the Writings. I did so, only to discover and to convince myself that there is no such animal. Oh yes, one can construe various important theological views that are strewn across these books—but a unified theology? I don't think so.

In fact, we might ask ourselves what we mean by biblical theology or Old Testament theology. Is this the same as the doctrine of God? A working definition might be the following: A systematic presentation of the biblical data about God and humans and the world according to biblical categories. There are thus two areas with which God would be concerned, human beings and the rest of God's creation. The third area, a big one, is God. Biblical data is dependent on what Bible or part of the Bible is being used. Systematic—there is the catch. This implies some kind of ordering and organization of the data. I don't think that this is really possible. There is no *one* biblical theology. There are many biblical theologies: the theology of the Chronicler, of Qoheleth, and so on. The insights of a particular "biblical theology" (by von Rad or others) may be useful and helpful for understanding the biblical data. However, the product is not a product of the Bible; it is the product of human intelligence and analysis of the Bible. Again, this is a worthwhile enterprise, and yields insight into the Bible. To repeat, within the Bible itself there are several theologies to be found, several construals of God. Deuteronomic theology, Priestly theology, the theology of the Yahwist—just to cite more examples of the broad range that exists within the Old Testament—are each different, with their own distinctive characteristics.

Within the Writings with which this little book is concerned, we have seen how many different roads have been travelled: the Chronicler, the Psalms, Daniel, and to include three books together: the wisdom literature. It is quite impossible to systematize all these into a unity.

Q. 99. You have been speaking of canonical and deuterocanonical throughout—what is the correct list of inspired books of the Bible?

This question has been answered at least implicitly in the first questions we raised (QQ. 1–3). All Christians have the same books that are found in the New Testament. The Jews and Protestants differ from Roman Catholics in their Old Testament; they are identical, but we Catholics have even more books, the deuterocanonicals (also called apocrypha).

But your question implies more than, who agrees with whom? A "correct" list, from the point of view of Roman Catholicism, was never official until it was issued at the Council of Trent. Previous to this time, variation was tolerated, although the Roman Catholic Church worked with the extra seven as a general rule. The uncertainty can be illustrated dramatically by the mild altercation between St. Jerome and St. Augustine. As is well known, Jerome translated the Hebrew Bible into Latin—the *Veritas Hebraica* (Hebrew truth) meant something to him. He was not happy about the prospect of the "other" books being included. However, St. Augustine admonished him that these books were read already in the Greek and Old Latin versions that were current. He did not want Jerome to go against this practice by excluding them. Unwillingly, Jerome went ahead to finish his translation, the "Catholic" canon that became known as the Vulgate translation that dominated western Europe for centuries. Jerome's work on the deuterocanonicals did not match the verve that characterized his work with the books written originally in Hebrew. For the most part, he seems to have revised a current Latin translation. His work formed the basis of the "Bible" in the Western world up to the time of the Reformation, and so became the yardstick for canonical works. Thus, the church published its list of books at the Council of Trent, declaring them as "sacred and canonical in their entirety, with all their parts, according to the text usually read in the Catholic Church and as they are in the ancient Latin Vulgate." Among "the parts" would be, for example, the story of the woman caught in adultery, John 7:53–8:11. The Vulgate was declared "authentic," in the juridical sense, i.e., juridically, free from error in faith and morals. The need to revise the Vulgate text in the direction of accuracy was readily acknowledged.

In a sense the church received the Old Testament from its Jewish mother. At the same time, it has to be said that the church's decision was its own. It was the Bible in its Greek (or Septuagint) form that was the basic Bible of the primitive church. Ultimately it was the usage of the Bible in the church, or church praxis, that led to a definitive final list. The practice in the Eastern (Orthodox) church has fluctuated over the centuries; by and large, it operates with a broader canon.

One also hears of the phrase, "canon within the canon." This means that in view of the recognition of divergent views within the Bible, one chooses basic documents to work with. Thus one can interpret the New Testament in the light of the doctrine of Galatians and Romans concerning faith. There is room for considerable dispute here. There is little profit to be gotten from opposing one New Testament view against another. Ultimately it is the consent of the church, with the aid of the study of scripture, that comes to a decision on the theological import. This does not create a hierarchy of inspiration among the books of the Bible. All of them are inspired, and we learn to move with them. We can all have our "favorites" among them, but if we limit ourselves to those, we impoverish both the Bible and ourselves.

Another phrase is receiving much attention in current thinking: "canonical shape." This means that one must pay attention to the Bible as transmitted to us, as a whole. For example, the genetic approach has been very much in vogue in the past. How did the present Bible take shape? Scholars have postulated various traditions which came together under guiding hands to form the Pentateuch. But it is the finished product (the Torah) that is the canonical shape, not the individual tradition, such as the Yahwist, or the Priestly traditions, which never existed, *as Bible*, within the people of God. Ultimately it is the Bible that one must deal with, and not some reconstruction, no matter how correct and insightful it is. As a reconstruction, it may contribute an insight into how our Bible came to be, but it is not yet the Bible. For more details, see B. Childs, *Introduction to the Old Testament as Scripture* (Philadelphia: Fortress, 1979).

Q. 100. Why should I, as a Christian, be concerned about the Writings?

An obvious reason is this: one cannot fully understand the New Testament literature without a basic knowledge of the Old Testament (for example, try reading the letter to the Hebrews). This point is made on the basic level of *understanding*. Christ and his followers were Jews; their Bible was the Hebrew Bible and it was out of this tradition that they were formed.

The second reason involves the stark difference between the testamental writings. The New Testament is familiar and thus to a certain extent "domesticated" for Christian taste. There is a whole history of twenty centuries of Christianity which has enlarged the biblical figure of God and God's people. The Old Testament is without the glossy aspect created by Christian tradition. For example, it plunges you directly into the hard core of reality in the matter of prayer. Just consider the realistic way in which the ancient Jew approached the Lord in prayer and in worship. There is nothing quite like the psalms, from which we can learn to be honest and frank in pouring out our feelings to God. Feelings of grief, of sinfulness, of anger, of praise, of questioning—the whole range of human emotions—are illumined by a thoughtful and empathetic reading of these prayers. The Old Testament is also a different world, one that is strange to us, and causes us to be more attentive to the ways of God with the people of God. One can grow as one absorbs the development in revelation throughout the Old Testament.

Third, the reading of the Old Testament is a normal way of progressing in Christian faith, as the liturgy selections for the eucharist (on Sundays and throughout the year) would indicate. In a certain sense, your question could be phrased, why read any Bible at all? As a Christian I believe in Christ and what my church teaches about him. Doesn't that suffice? I cannot deny that, but the real question is this: will not your faith grow under the impulse of the Holy Spirit as you read and meditate on the Bible? Everyone needs some inspiration in life, and the Bible is one of the main sources of spiritual growth.

Other reasons can be adduced, but they mean little unless one is prepared to make time for Bible reading. Conviction about the importance and value of it will help one's resolve to persevere.

Q. 101. What is your favorite book among the Writings?

That is a very difficult question to answer. Any choice is highly personal, and may not be appropriate for others. I think I would choose the psalms. They are filled with faith, imagination, and literary power. Naturally, some appeal more than others. On the whole, they wield a more powerful influence than any of the other Writings. However, I thought of replying to your question by saying, "the wisdom books" i.e., Proverbs, Job, and Qoheleth. But your question states "favorite book." In one sense, these three are one: they are all books that deal with human wisdom and thus together they make a rather complete statement about human experience and God. They illustrate everyday experience, and pose to us the question of the role of God in our daily lives. It is here (as well as in certain psalms; cf. Pss 88 and 73) that the burning question of God's treatment of human beings arises—a problem with which we still struggle.

INDEX OF SUBJECTS TREATED
IN THE QUESTIONS

(The numbers listed below refer to Questions, not to pages.)

Other Books in the Series

RESPONSES TO 101 QUESTIONS ON THE BIBLE
by Raymond E. Brown, S.S.

RESPONSES TO 101 QUESTION ON THE
DEAD SEA SCROLLS
by Joseph A. Fitzmyer, S.J.

RESPONSES TO 101 QUESTIONS ABOUT JESUS
by Michael L. Cook, S.J.

RESPONSES TO 101 QUESTIONS ABOUT FEMINISM
by Denise Lardner Carmody